Sitting
in the
Bay
Window

A Book for Parents
of Young Alcoholics

• • •

Jack Mumey

Contemporary Books, Inc.
Chicago

Library of Congress Cataloging in Publication Data

Mumey, Jack.
    Sitting in the bay window.

    Includes index.
    1. Youth—United States—Alcohol use.   2. Youth—
United States—Family relationships.   3. Alcoholics—
United States—Family relationships.   I. Title.
HV5135.M86   1984   362.8'2   84-17010
ISBN 0-8092-5418-2

Published by Contemporary Books, Inc.
180 North Michigan Avenue, Chicago, Illinois 60601
Manufactured in the United States of America
Library of Congress Catalog Card Number: 84-17010
International Standard Book Number: 0-8092-5418-2

Published simultaneously in Canada by Beaverbooks, Ltd.
195 Allstate Parkway, Valleywood Business Park
Markham, Ontario L3R 4T8 Canada

• • •
Contents

In the spirit of what was intended, this book belongs to:

Megan Judith

"The torch has been passed. . . ."

John F. Kennedy
Inaugural Address
January 20, 1961

Carry it well!

Preface

This is a book about love: the love of parents for children; the love of parents for each other; and the love of learning to get well together.

The moment this book took form in my mind can be pinpointed as precisely as the route on a sea captain's chart. When one of my patients talked of her hours of "sitting in her bay window" in anguish and concern over her alcoholic daughter, I took a small piece of paper from my shirt pocket and jotted down the phrase *sitting in the bay window*. At that very moment this book was born.

To say that more than two years of listening and talking with parents has been productive is an understatement. It has been the backbone of what you are about to read and, I hope, from which you are about to learn. For reasons of confidentiality, all of the names have been fictionalized, as well as the cases or scenarios that I have used to illustrate certain points.

The parents I have been privileged to know and to work with at our Gateway Treatment Center will undoubtedly recognize themselves or draw some similarities between themselves and the parents discussed here. For that, I offer no apology. We are dealing with human emotions—with all of the things, as Shakespeare said, "that flesh is heir to"—and the gamut of feelings that must be run by parents are not limited. They transcend locale, names, places, facts, and we use them to deal with the things that life has dealt.

As a parent myself, I always feel a step behind, inadequate when the skinned knees of a three-year-old become the deep anguish of a twenty-three-year-old. When the mass of tricycle and limbs on the sidewalk becomes a mass of hurt and emotion, it is then that I need to call on my "daddy wings" for the support I need.

For it is in being "daddy" or "mommy" that the true expectations of parenthood are met. It's too easy to say, "You're all grown up now; solve your own problems!" When the main problem to be solved is alcohol or other drug abuse, then and really then do parents need a lifeline.

It all seems so overwhelming, so endless, and the feeling of being "out there all alone" becomes overpowering. That's why this book was written. You are not alone. There *is* help and there *is* hope!

Many other books for parents of alcoholics are available to the reader. Clinical help abounds, and a search of the libraries in your town will yield a wealth of such information. In this book, however, readers will find more of a day-by-day how-to approach to dealing with *themselves* when alcoholism strikes.

The arguments in this book about THIQ and genetic inheritance are just that—arguments. For more information on genetics and alcohol abuse, turn to a more clinical or technical source. Here, the issue is discussed only as a factor in accenting alcoholism as a disease.

A basic premise of this book is that alcoholism must be accepted for what it is: a disease that is among the most rank and deadly that we encounter in our time on earth.

Whatever we learn, whatever strides we make in our lifetimes, will be for the ultimate good of all children now living and those yet to be born, who may face the undeniable agony of having been given the disease by mere fact of having no choice in their parenthood.

May the torch be passed to them clean and burning bright, not clouded or smoking from incalculable hurt, agony, and physical pain. May the torch be passed with firm hands, not those shaking from alcohol withdrawal; with firm purpose for what life is meant to be and not what life has been, living from one damnable drink to the next.

To all parents who have faced and will face this problem, this book is humbly inscribed.

• • •
Acknowledgments

Thanks to my colleagues at Gateway Treatment Center, Aurora, Colorado. Their patience with picking up additional burdens while I "run off to write" is, it seems, inexhaustible.

To my partner Paul Staley I owe particularly deep gratitude. He has always made time available for discussion with me, even though his own schedule was jammed, especially since the arrival of a first child to him and his lovely and supportive wife, Sandy. They both have continued to be there for me in especially difficult times.

Fellow therapist John Mullan took it upon himself to keep my humor level at the peak, not allowing me to get too serious about myself—something I find easier to do as a book gets further along.

My running partner Liz Telford, a fine therapist and fine lady, has provided me with much insight into certain sections of this book. Her continual "nagging," on and off the running paths, helped me meet deadlines and keep goals in sight.

• • • Acknowledgments • • •

My editor, Shari Lesser, is what every author should have: a combination of gentle persuader and tough task-master, who provided encouragement, insight, and, above all, iron-fist objectivity.

The family of any author suffers untold agonies, having to put up with the writer before, during, and after the creative process. Mine has been exemplary in all aspects, constantly full of encouragement, even when I was doing all that was humanly possible to resign from the "Mister Nice Guy" category of life!

Night after night I find myself sitting in the bay window of our living room. I just sit there on the big cushions watching the cars drive up and down our street. I sit there and wonder if the next car will be my daughter coming home drunk, or whether it will be the police with a message for us. . . .

A mother of an alcoholic youngster

1

• • •

Let's Get
Acquainted!

As parents of an alcoholic, you know that your child's actions, reactions, and behavior patterns don't only affect him or her. They affect your entire family—mother, father, brothers, sisters, grandma, grandpa, aunts, and uncles—as well as friends and others who care.

You feel stumped. You feel hurt, angry, miserable, and powerless to do anything beyond lecturing your son or daughter, grounding him or her, taking away the car, suspending allowance, or trying the other weak tools you have tried in your frustrating battle to keep your youngster away from alcohol.

In short, you need help, and that's okay! That's what this book is all about—help! So many families don't want to "air their dirty linen" in front of anyone else, so the idea of family therapy, family treatment, counselors, therapists, social workers, and psychologists strikes some kind of unknown terror in their hearts.

Well, together, we can dispel some of those bugaboos, and help you to see that the family in treatment for the disease of alcoholism is the family with the very best chance of getting well and staying well.

More and more, alcoholism experts pound away at this theme: The family in treatment together, stays together. As parents, you need to learn new tools for coping, new mechanisms that can be shifted into place to restore your sanity so you can begin to regain some semblance of order in your lives.

Throughout this book we will talk about therapy and counseling, treatment and treatment centers. You are probably already aware of Alcoholics Anonymous, that worldwide self-help organization that has guided so many millions back on the road to recovery. However, you may not know as much about where to go for treatment as a family, or even why you need to seek this kind of professional help.

We can answer the "where" part now; I hope that when you have read this book, and you begin to use the tools that are being offered, you will understand the "why" of family treatment.

In your telephone directory, there is a listing for "Community Services," and one of the categories listed is that of "Mental Health." This listing will give you the names of one or more public health organizations, many of them maintaining a 24-hour telephone number, where you can seek immediate response to your questions, your fears, and your best course of action. The 24-hour hotline number of AA also offers referrals to other sources.

The Yellow Pages of your telephone directory carry a listing under "Alcoholism Information and Treatment Centers." Here, you will find many treatment centers, both inpatient (in a hospital setting) and outpatient, residential treatment centers (halfway houses or rehabilitation centers), and individuals who specialize in the treatment of alcoholism. All of these resources will assist you in getting help as a family, including strong cross-referrals to Al-

Anon, the support arm for the members of an alcoholic's family.

Help is out there in great quantities; all you have to do is seek it! Not everything that you are going to read about in these pages is going to work, so let's get that on the table between us right now. When you are dealing with a complex and baffling disease like alcoholism, and even with excessive drinking and "problem drinking," you are swimming in a vast ocean of uncertainty. What seems to work for one person doesn't work at all for someone else.

I think particularly of the many people who tell us at Gateway Treatment Center that "so-and-so got sober *strictly* through AA," or "so-and-so just made up his or her mind to stop drinking, and *did!*" Both true statements in many thousands of cases, and both commendable courses of action neither of which will get any argument from me. My personal philosophy is *"whatever works, do it!"*

I feel strongly that the alcoholic and family need to treat the disease together. In conjunction with life-long support that is available through AA, you get a winning combination to help keep the alcoholism in remission. That's why I'm up front with you right here. Not everything is going to work and perhaps you will find all too often that failure stands in your way, keeping you from helping your young alcoholic find his or her sobriety, forcing you back into therapy and treatment.

But back you must go! You must believe in, and trust the process of getting well. Failure after failure may make you want to throw up your hands in despair and say, "I've had it! I can't take any more!" But you can . . . and you will. You will continue, as parents, to explore every possible avenue that leads to recovery, because you love the person afflicted with the disease.

It is absolutely vital that you be prepared to get help for yourselves, even if the young person you care about so much refuses all attempts at treatment. When things *do* fail, then the support of Alcoholics Anonymous, particularly Al-Anon, will be a readily available source of help. Turn to the front of your telephone directory and you will find 24-hour numbers for these organizations.

Treatment for the whole family is available through countless sources. You *can* go to treatment centers as parents, and if they don't have groups specifically for you, they will have individual and couple therapy, and in many instances, will know of an ongoing support group somewhere else.

Throughout these pages you will find a particular drug, *Antabuse*, mentioned. This is a brand name of the drug *disulfiram*, and is a prescription drug that is used oftentimes as another tool in the management of the alcoholic patient.

It is a crutch, an aid only, since the taking of Antabuse will not make it safe for the alcoholic to drink. Quite the contrary. It is a drug that blocks the metabolizing process of the alcohol in the system, preventing it from going beyond the poisonous state that it is when first taken, to the chemical conversion that sedates the brain and provides the temporary "high" one gets from drinking.

When people on Antabuse try to drink alcohol, or come into prolonged contact with alcohol through creams, aftershaves, perfumes, etc., they become violently ill and, perhaps, suffer fatal consequences. The physician and treatment team that is administering Antabuse to your alcoholic will thoroughly explain the dangers of trying to drink on Antabuse.

You will learn in these chapters that you are not responsible for your child's actions when he or she is taking Antabuse. However, you certainly will not want to serve things that contain alcohol, possibly causing an adverse reaction to the Antabuse.

Finally, you needn't have a diagnosed alcoholic in your family in order to use this book. If you are the parents of a "problem drinker," an "episodic" or "binge" drinker (one who goes on drinking sprees in spurts as opposed to regular, daily drinking), or you find yourself too frequently pacing the floors at night, worrying about your child, I believe you will find help in these pages.

If nothing else, I hope this book will urge you to face the problem of alcohol abuse squarely, to get an assessment by a professional, to confront the issue together as a family, and, as a family, to get the kind of help and support you so desperately need.

Well, now, that should do it! Let's move on to the understanding of the disease, and the role parents play in its treatment. Let's look at the tools, experiences, and suggestions that can help you get out of your own bay window and back on solid ground with the young alcoholic you love so much.

2
• • •
Support
for Parents

This book is intended to help parents deal with the day-to-day problems of living with an alcoholic child. As such, it emphasizes the steps that parents can take to help their kids handle the disease of alcoholism. But essential to the recovery of the youngster is the parents' acceptance of the fact that the entire family of the alcohol abuser needs to get well.

In order to help the young alcoholic or alcohol abuser in your family, you must consider what's important for you as parents. You too need support, and plenty of it is available. Too often it is assumed that parents don't need any help because they can handle the problem on their own or that, because the alcohol issue is "really the problem of the abuser in the family," any help should be given to that individual alone. Both of these points of view are wrong. The family gets sick together, and they *must* get well together!

PARENTS' GROUPS

Our parents' group at Gateway Treatment Center is a good example of folks getting well for themselves. In the more than two years that the group has been meeting weekly, we have had only a few long-term dropouts.

Many of these mothers and fathers no longer have any young people in treatment for one reason or another, yet they continue to be a part of their own support group. What they do better than anyone else is carry the message to other parents who are going through the shame, anger, guilt, and denial of a family alcohol or other drug problem.

The importance of having peer group support cannot be overemphasized. It's far easier to carry a shared burden. Hardly any new problems are revealed in group; mostly we hear about the same kinds of problems in different settings.

When a new couple enters our parents' group, they come in feeling as if they have a totally unique problem. It is not very long into their group sessions, however, before their knowing smiles express recognition—they've heard this story before—and they are relieved to hear their peers tell of similar experiences.

The names and places are different, but the events related by a distraught mother and/or father seem painfully familiar. There is a healing in just being in the same room with other parents who are experiencing the same feelings as you, in the understanding that you are not alone, that you do not have to suffer in silence.

As a bonus, group meetings are more than just therapy sessions; they are wonderful social events as well. Hardly a week goes by in our group without someone bringing in a big batch of chocolate chip cookies, homemade fudge, or other such delicacies. It's tough on the waistline, but it's wonderful for the camaraderie that has developed!

Some of the members of our group have made it a regular practice to get together for lunch every other week or so, working that event around their work schedules. While they may have started out having only one thing in common, an alcoholic young adult, they have quickly expanded their interests to include many varied topics.

If there are no treatment centers in your area that offer such parents' groups, there is Al-Anon, run by Alcoholics Anonymous, a wonderful opportunity for family members of the alcoholic to engage in meaningful dialogue with other family members who are suffering from the effects of the disease. Or you may attend open AA meetings with your alcoholic.

Start Your Own Group

If your family is already in therapy with a counselor, the counselor and/or his colleagues may already have formed a parents' group. If not, take a tip from your days as den mother, homeroom leader, scoutmaster, or youth group worker and organize your own group.

Remember when you were asked to "put something together" even if there didn't seem to be the slightest interest in forming a group or a pack, or a den, or a school pageant? You got busy and, somehow, did it!

The natural abilities that made other people aware of your leadership qualities then haven't deserted you now. Look around you at the other parents who seem to be just dropping off their young people to keep an appointment with a counselor or another professional.

Be bold! Be brave! Introduce yourself: "Excuse me! I'm John Doe, and I've noticed that every time we bring our son here you and your wife are dropping someone off, too. Our son is in treatment for an alcohol problem, and we are trying to find other parents to talk with. Are you interested?"

If that sounds too pushy (it doesn't quite fit your style), try a low-key approach: "Excuse me. John Doe's the name. My wife and I are looking for help with our son's alcohol problem. Is there a group at this place for parents?"

The point is, try anything as an ice breaker. What you want to do is get a group started that can be mutually helpful to all concerned. You can do it! I don't care how naturally shy you are or how difficult it may be for you to talk to strangers. The importance of your mission has to overcome all that. Just remember that scout troop you started when everyone else said there was no interest. Remember that school play you did when "everyone" told you that parents wouldn't take the time or put in the energy to help make it go!

Well, this is far more serious. You'll want support for yourselves so badly that you will find amazing new skills that you didn't think you had! Once you are successful in identifying other interested parents, you can seek a counselor or therapist to help you facilitate the group.

The parents with whom I've worked over the years have developed such keen insights and skills that they are able to help the new people in their group every bit as effectively as the group leader. They run their own group with a great deal of enthusiasm, leaving the therapist free to observe and help them discover other behaviors about themselves that may be contributing to their problems with an alcoholic youngster.

The Ongoing Group

An important point to keep in mind concerning parents' groups is that they can remain active to provide support as long as it is needed. Parents use such groups as a means of keeping a check on their emotional temperatures long after initial treatment has been completed. Recovery from the disease of alcoholism is a lifelong process and never ends! If there is a period of "letting down," the old tapes will start to play and the old patterns will reemerge, plunging you and the rest of the family back into trouble. Count on it! You don't have to waste time testing the theory; it's been done before you and proven over and over that the family that lapses into laziness with their aftercare will soon be back for *active* treatment for the same problems.

9

What I suggest, if you have completed an active treatment program of some kind and have no group going to provide weekly support, is a parental "spring tune-up." Gather your family members, make an appointment, and go back in together for a professional reevaluation of how you're doing. You might get a clean bill of health, or the therapist might pick up on a trouble spot that he or she will want to call to your attention. Again, what you do about it is up to you. The old "a stitch in time" adage certainly holds true with the principle of follow-up therapy and aftercare counseling for parents as well as for the alcoholic or alcohol abuser.

FAMILY THERAPY

Too often family members of an alcoholic, particularly parents, let their anger get in the way of helping the whole family. They conclude that because the problem really isn't theirs, they don't need to expend the effort toward getting well. This attitude prevents them from seeking treatment help and certainly reduces the alcoholic's motivation to work on his or her problem.

In treatment parents will be led through a process through which they can learn about the disease and about their part in the recovery process. *Treatment begins the moment the family realizes it has a problem and decides to seek help.*

There is nothing more gratifying to see than parents who have realized the benefits of family therapy. They think in a more logical pattern; they behave more rationally (something they may have almost forgotten how to do); and they begin to get rid of that old bugaboo, *guilt.*

Family therapy also gives everyone, not just the alcoholic, an equal chance to get well. I think this is important for parents. It's too easy for parents to "bite the bullet" and say to each other, "It doesn't really matter about *us!*"

Rubbish! It matters a great deal! If you don't care about yourselves, you will simply end up making the same mistakes with the next kid in line, who may end up with the same problem. For you to be in therapy, as a couple or as a single parent, is an *essential* part of your growth in dealing with this alcohol problem. Don't let the cost of therapy stop you. There are trained people who will work with you regardless of your financial station in life. Like nurses and other health care professionals, the majority of alcohol counselors and therapists put their own monetary interests far behind their work.

For the therapist nothing begins to match the reward of seeing a sick family leave treatment with a "wellness glow." No amount of money can ever begin to match that particular feeling. My colleagues and I have stood in the background of many graduation ceremonies for people leaving our treatment center and assured each other that our payoff is to see these folks leaving hand in hand, happy victors over alcoholism.

The conjoint therapy approach, in which you and your young alcoholic are in counseling together, meeting weekly with a counselor, can open many doors in the treatment of the family of an alcoholic.

The four of you—parents, child, and counselor—alone in one room, are able to confront each other in a controlled atmosphere so things can be discussed instead of shouted about. It makes a tremendous difference, and you will realize the value of such sessions from the very beginning.

Again, don't throw up your hands and say, "We can't afford it!" You'd better think instead of whether you can afford *not* to have these sessions. Your local mental health center or another such public organization will help you find something that will fit your pocketbook.

Don't let foolish pride stand in your way, either. More good parents and their alcohol-abusing young adults have gone down the emotional drain because they failed to seek help, insisting, "We can do it ourselves, privately, without a stranger!" or "We don't have to air our dirty linen in front of someone else; we've always solved our own problems before!"

11

It's this kind of archaic thinking that can get you into real trouble and keep you there. It makes as much sense to try to solve your family's alcohol problem alone as it does to do your own appendectomy or remove the tonsils of your youngest child!

Professional help is required to bring you and your young person together just to begin talking again. It's not a luxury but a necessity because of the specialized nature of the disease. Today, many religious denominations have provided trained counselors for their congregations. These are dedicated men and women who have invested many hours of training and many dollars (generally from limited funds) to earn their certification as trained alcohol/drug abuse counselors. Parents and their young abusers can get this kind of counseling for the mere cost of asking for the help!

A SHOULDER TO LEAN ON

Let's say that you've followed the advice given so far in this chapter, and you've sought family therapy and joined a parents' group. Well, there's one more source of comfort and support that's never far away—your spouse. Think about the two of you for just a moment. Try to remember the last time you sat down together and really talked. It can be kind of scary to know that it's been weeks or even months. When the immediate crisis was dealt with and the alcohol problem put to rest, did you also put yourselves on hold as a couple? I'll bet you did!

At this point your situation resembles those times when your kids were very young and a serious illness struck. Perhaps you were in the middle of some marital difficulties of your own. But you put those aside and jumped in to handle the crisis *together*. Whatever the problem was, it took an immediate backseat to your care and concern for the ill child. That's the way it should be, and that's the way it has been while you've been working with the alcohol problem. You have been busy dealing with the immediate

12

welfare of the abusing youngster, without giving a lot of thought to where the two of you were headed as a couple.

It's essential now that you keep a firm finger on the emotional pulse of both of you. You have come through tough times in learning to cope with alcoholism, and when the immediate crisis has passed (just as when the fever broke for the sick little child), you may be tempted to pick up the marital difficulties again.

If you have a firm understanding of this, you can avoid the pitfalls and keep yourselves moving along a healthy path. You have to put your own marriage difficulties (if any) aside in order to deal with the immediate crisis of alcoholism or alcohol abuse by one of your children.

Now that the crisis is passed, you may be tempted to reopen the difficulties between you again. This is natural because you didn't resolve those difficulties; you merely set them aside. Sooner or later they will have to be dealt with, and for you as a couple to enter conjoint therapy or some form of marriage counseling can be extremely helpful.

Again, don't be embarrassed to seek help. Be open and frank with each other about the needs you have and the best ways to get help, as well as the best place.

You will know when the family is beginning to return to "normal" when it becomes OK to talk openly about what's wrong with it. When you can laugh and cry in each other's company without fear or shame, you will know that you are giving each other permission to grow in your own ways! The free exchange of views among mother, father, and all children, including the alcoholic, will make for a much stronger lifeline for recovery from the disease.

Forgiving each other will be an important part of support for you, as parents. Not only does it behoove you to forgive each other; it will also pay off for you to begin to forgive *yourself.*

You were not to be expected to know or even to realize when the drug of alcohol took over in your young adult's life, particularly since denial of the problem is such a major part of the disease. You were used to "turning the other cheek" in addition to just plain turning your head away so as not to see what was happening.

Many times I have heard mothers and fathers bemoan in group, "If I had only *known!*" or "How *could* I have been so stupid?!"

These are the remarks of parents who are unwilling to admit they are human, with all the foibles and flaws of all human beings. It's time to gain support—through therapy, parents' groups, and communication with each other—for yourself and for what you have done right instead of wrong.

PARENTS' SUPPORT CHECKLIST

The seven points below can remind you of the constant need to get the support that will allow you to continue dealing with what the disease of alcoholism has done to you as parents. Your participation in open AA meetings with your alcoholic and in Al-Anon meetings and other groups for yourselves can help keep these points in focus.

1. Is there a parents' group for us where our alcoholic is being treated?
2. Are we willing to form such a group in order to pass the message to other parents about getting well?
3. Will we enter conjoint therapy with our alcoholic?
4. Will we seek therapy for ourselves as a couple?
5. Are we ready to forgive ourselves?
6. Do we realize that recovery is a *lifelong* process?
7. Can we continue to talk openly as a family?

Keep yourselves strong and healthy! You will *gain* support by *giving* support—to your spouse, to your alcoholic, to fellow members of your group, who are parents themselves.

'Tis not enough to help the feeble up,
But to support him after.

Shakespeare
(*Timon of Athens*)

3
• • •
Meet the Disease

"What do you mean, disease? The kid's *drunk*!"

"Disease, my foot! You get a grip on yourself or *I'll* show you disease!"

"You can do it! Just put your shoulder to the wheel, and make up your mind to quit drinking!"

"You come from good stock; there's no *disease* in our family background!"

And so it goes. Countless confrontations between parents and their offspring to explain away a severe *family* problem—alcoholism. These misguided notions that family strength comes from who you are and the way you've been brought up—the *moral* fiber of the family—are very prevalent among parents facing the heartbreak of alcoholism or alcohol abuse by a younger member of the family. And why not? For centuries man has survived on an attitude that says, "If you want to do something strongly enough, you just *do* it!"

Your own ancestors may have hacked their way through the Oregon wilderness or rolled bandages in the Revolutionary War. They also could have been alcoholic and passed on that disease through many generations to you and yours.

That's genetic inheritance, and we are all beneficiaries of certain genetic traits. Your blue eyes or red hair, his olive complexion or big feet—these are everyday examples of genetic inheritance. And so is alcoholism!

It seems perfectly OK to accept obvious physical traits of inheritance like those just mentioned; the big feet, up-turned nose, and sparkling blue eyes all fall into a family's "it can't be helped" category. But when you begin to talk about alcoholism, most parents just can't swallow the fact that they may have to deal with a *disease.* This is perfectly natural. If it is a disease, then it is you, the parent, who passed it along to your offspring, and you may not have even the slightest drinking problem!

Well, you can be assured that it *is* a disease. Way back in 1774, while your great-great-great grandmother was rolling those bandages for the boys at Bunker Hill, a doctor friend of Ben Franklin was hard at work thinking about the link between alcohol abuse and the deterioration of the body.

Dr. Benjamin Rush was the preeminent physician of his time, earning many honors in his lifetime and founding Dickinson College. He was known in later years as the "father of American temperance" for his many publications of tract material on the evils of drink. But first and foremost, he was a physician and greatly concerned with what was becoming painfully clear to him: there was a definite link between the deterioration of mind and body and the overuse (abuse) of "spirituous liquors."

It is Rush who can be credited with first correctly identifying alcoholism as a disease, and his learned paper of scientific inquiry into the effects of alcohol on the mind and body of human beings remains a guideline for serious students of the disease of alcoholism.

Rush learned that alcoholism is much more physiologically oriented than had been previously believed, and he advanced the theory that there is a direct *chemical* effect on the human body.

In 1964 the American Medical Association, after years of intensive research, came to the same conclusion and recognized alcoholism as a disease.

You can apply the same criteria to alcoholism that are applied to most major diseases. First, you can identify alcoholism as a *primary* disease. That is, it isn't caused by something else. It's a disease all on its own. You don't "catch" alcoholism! Second, the disease is *treatable*. We can't *cure* alcoholism, but it can be treated. This is very similar to the disease of diabetes. It can be *treated*, but so far, it can't be cured. The third element in our diagnosis is *progression*. Alcoholism is a *progressive* disease; it gets worse, not better, as it goes along untreated. As I tell clients, alcoholism is like pregnancy: one rarely gets *smaller* in the fourth or fifth month of pregnancy! Finally, the clincher is that alcoholism, when left untreated, is *fatal.* You die from it, plain and simple. Alcoholism is a life-threatening disease. So these four elements clearly put alcoholism in the same category with other diseases, such as cancer and diabetes.

As a recovering alcoholic I find this factor fairly comforting. It's good to know that I have a *disease* instead of some weak link in personal character or lack of gumption to quit drinking! That's why it's so important for you as a parent to understand that you must stop attacking the morality of the drinking issue and begin fighting back with facts and understanding. You surely would not be embarrassed at your son or daughter having, say, an asthma attack, even in public. Most of you, however, are utterly devastated by a drinking incident involving your children.

This is completely understandable. The drunken person, young or old, is not a pretty sight. When the person is younger, it can be even more disgusting. No parent who loves his or her child would refuse to help, particularly in times of sickness. Why, then, do so many parents find it impossible to break through barriers of prejudice when it comes to alcohol abuse? I believe the answer is *fear*, plain and simple. We don't wish to believe that our child could be mentally and physically disposed not to be able to handle alcohol in a responsible manner. And so we are afraid, and we retreat into absolute denial.

There is no need for this unbridled fear once you can understand and accept the disease concept of alcoholism and the role of the parent in its genetic chain. Parental guilt need not be a factor here, for the simple truth is that none of us had any say in choosing our parents! If we have inherited certain traits, certain genetic factors, then we have, and there's not a whole lot that can be done about that. As a parent you have simply been the latest link in the genetic chain to carry certain factors forward into the present generation.

THE THIQ FACTOR

One of the factors you *may* have passed along to your children is called the *THIQ factor*. Dr. David Ohlms, an eminent psychiatrist, presents this concept in the clearest fashion.

THIQ is a handy abbreviation for a very addictive substance, perhaps the *most* addictive substance known to man: tetrahydroisoquinoline. Now you know why we just say "THIQ." THIQ is an alkaloid produced in the brain when some very strange and mysterious genetic chemistry takes place.

When any of us drink alcohol we are drinking poison! Ethyl alcohol is poison, and it is our liver that must be called into action to do some quick cleansing and metabolizing to turn the poison into sugar. A drink of alcohol is quickly divested of ammonia, acetic acid, and uric acid. When we drink it, the alcohol cannot remain in its state of toxicity; it must be converted, or *everyone* could die on the spot. The alcohol becomes acetaldehyde, perhaps the most dangerous of man's poisons. Mother Nature converts the acetaldehyde into acetic acid, commonly known as vinegar.

This toned-down alcohol eventually leaves the body through water (urine) and carbon dioxide.

Here's where genetics start playing a vital role. For some unknown reason, when the acetaldehyde is formed from the alcohol, a small amount seeps into a neurotransmitter in the brain called *dopamine*. Everyone has neurotransmitters; we can't live without them. In the process, the dopamine, in combination with this small amount of acetaldehyde, goes through a lot of chemical reactions that are too complicated to explain here. Anyway, what is formed from this liaison are many alkaloids. Among those alkaloids is THIQ. THIQ remains in the brain for a lifetime. It is a hair-triggered gun that demands alcohol and remains in a state of readiness to jump into action at the merest hint of alcohol's presence in the system.

The analogy of a loaded mousetrap can help explain this THIQ danger. Many times you set two mousetraps under a kitchen sink, determined to get the little vermin that are eating away in your kitchen. And you are successful! In the middle of the night you may hear the trap being sprung, and you know you got the intruder.

You'll empty the trap and leave the second one sitting there, forgotten. Sometimes for weeks the mousetrap sits under the sink, waiting for the mouse that never shows up. You forget all about it until some bright cheery morning when you are down on your hands and knees, rummaging in the cupboard under the sink, looking for that lost scouring pad. Suddenly, *wham!* You hit the forgotten trap and it goes off, causing you to raise your head in fright, bang same head on the cabinet edge, and turn the surrounding air blue!

The trap has remained loaded. Oh, the cheese may have shrunk a bit, or maybe it is even no longer in the trap. But the deadly spring has remained cocked, and you were able to set it off after many weeks of inactivity. That's how THIQ behaves in the brain of the alcoholic. Once it has been manufactured it remains there, loaded, ready to trigger the need for alcohol in addictive doses.

Here's the clincher for genetic alcoholism. This THIQ factor is found *only* in the brains of alcoholics and heroin addicts! It is *not* in the brain of the normal social drinker. How did it get in the brains of alcoholics in the first place? It was passed on through the family generations just like the blue eyes or the big feet! Virginia Davis, a scientist working on brain cancers, discovered this tie-in when she was finding measurable amounts of THIQ in the brains of newly deceased skid-row alcoholics. Up to this point THIQ was known only to exist in heroin addicts.

Many, many tests were conducted over a long period of time in which THIQ was injected into the brains of rats who were absolutely aversive to alcohol. That is, the rats would die before they would touch water tainted with even the slightest amount of alcohol. The rats were known to thirst to death before they would drink alcohol. After injecting the THIQ into the rats' brains, however, the same alcohol-avoiding animals would drink pure vodka! They would drink themselves to death!

Scientists were soon able to breed a strain of totally alcoholic rats by inbreeding with other rats. A few generations previous these animals had been totally abstinent. The enormity of this discovery can hardly be measured in its importance to families of alcoholics.

As parents you can understand that you may have transmitted this THIQ factor to your children, even though you may not abuse alcohol or even drink yourself.

Once this THIQ factor is in the brain it remains there for life. How do we know this? Because scientists injected THIQ into monkeys. Some animals were slaughtered within a few hours of the injections. Others were allowed to live for seven years or more. When these animals were killed and autopsied they had the same amounts of THIQ in their brains as had been injected on the very first day. The THIQ had grown in neither volume nor potency. But it was *still there.*

This is another point of comfort for me as a recovering alcoholic, and it should help you, too. I know that every alcoholic has this "loaded mousetrap" in his or her brain and that it can be triggered again even after prolonged years of sobriety. All it takes is one drink, and in a matter of hours or days or weeks the alcoholic will go right back to drinking, and probably even *harder* than before, as if the drinking had never stopped for all those years.

The THIQ had remained, loaded for action in the monkey's brain for those seven years; it remains loaded in my brain and in the brain of all other alcoholics.

I said this was a point of comfort for me. Why? Because I know the risks and don't have to experiment or wonder what would happen if I started to take "just one little drink" again after whatever period of sobriety. I *know* the gun is loaded. That THIQ factor will still be there, and that "one little drink" will activate the chemical reaction all over again.

The point is, if I *know* the consequences, the outcome is predictable and I don't have to experiment with it!

Where did I get this THIQ factor? Most likely from my mother. She died from injuries received in an automobile accident. She was a passenger in a car struck head-on. But she died from internal bleeding, from the inability of her alcoholic liver to function. My mother was an alcoholic, and probably there have been other members of my family whom we could label *alcoholic*. I certainly remember a grandfather and a natural father who had serious alcohol problems.

As a parent, what does this do for me? Make me feel guilty that I have passed along my THIQ factor to my four children and my children's children as they come along? Absolutely not! My children are all very much aware of the alcoholism strain in the family, and as a result they accept the adult responsibility for their own actions.

This is where you, as a parent of an alcoholic child, have to start. It becomes essential for you to do a little detective work on your own family background.

Yes, *you* will have to do your own alcoholism investigation. The scientific study of alcoholism is not yet so advanced that you can walk into the nearest medical lab and simply request that you be "tested" for the predisposition toward alcoholism. The only way to test for THIQ currently is to extract brain fluid during an autopsy. Consequently, it behooves you to search your family background for signs of alcohol abuse. In the name of caution and prevention, you can assume that the THIQ factor is present in your family's genetic makeup if you can find evidence of alcoholism in your progenitors.

How can you pinpoint the alcoholic or alcohol abuser in your family? Don't be afraid to talk to other family members. Draw them out and try to locate the first appearance of the THIQ factor in your family line. The key message here is to stop feeling guilty and start getting on with doing something about your role in this alcohol business. (We'll talk more about guilt in Chapter 4.)

For now, be at ease with two important points from this chapter:

1. There is strong medical, scientific evidence to support the disease concept of alcoholism. It is recognized worldwide as such.

2. By just being who you are, a member of a specific family, you may have inherited a genetic disorder called the THIQ factor, which has predisposed you and your offspring to alcohol abuse and perhaps alcoholism.

ACCEPTING YOUR HERITAGE

You can see that the ability to "put the shoulder to the wheel" or "keep a stiff upper lip" and all the other traditional family mottos that have served you well have very little to do with combating alcoholism. It may seem to help you as a parent to think that an extra amount of willpower bred from good old New England stock or wonderful Southern gentility is going to contribute significantly to solving the problem, but I assure you it won't!

This isn't to say that family background and strong moral

fiber aren't important. They certainly are. However, it makes as much sense to say that "character," "upbringing," and "family tradition" will prevent the alcoholic from drinking as to say the diabetic won't have any more problems because the family sold the candy store.

As soon as the parents begin to treat the problem as a disease they will begin to make some sense from the chaos that may have overtaken their family life.

This is not to say that other factors can't play an important role in the development of the alcoholic. They most certainly can. There is a psychological addiction that builds along with the physical addiction to the drug, and both of these elements require equal treatment for successful remission of the disease. If you are the parent of a moody young adult who becomes animated only when he or she drinks, then whoever is treating your young person will look at all the secondary psychological factors that are being hidden by the use of alcohol.

It is natural to rebel against the disease concept of alcoholism, because no one likes to think he or she has been responsible for delivering a less than perfect youngster into the world. It's only human nature to want to believe that you have only perfect genetic qualities, and something like the THIQ factor is totally at odds with your self-image. But it's much easier on your parenthood to accept the fact that many of our diseases involve genetics to some extent.

Except for diseases that can be pinpointed as viruses, such as tuberculosis or infantile paralysis, we don't really know what causes most diseases. Science is still searching for answers to questions posed by the THIQ factor. Might it be possible to find a method to extract brain fluid safely to test for THIQ while a person is living? Is the newfound ability to tap the amniotic fluid of an unborn child to test the level of alcohol in the fetus's system a first step toward this goal? Very possibly.

Laboratories around the world are studying possible methods to prevent the chemical reaction that converts acetaldehyde into dopamine from taking place at all. Every

23

so often a new discovery is announced that ties another link into the genetic chain of alcoholism, and it is my belief that, through the marvels of genetic engineering, someday babies will be conceived and born without this THIQ factor.

In the meantime, what's wrong with accepting, as parents, that this genetic deficiency just possibly *could* exist? I once had a woman tell me after a lecture to alcoholic patients at a local hospital that she couldn't buy this theory of an inherited disease.

"Why not?" I asked. "Tell me about your family, please."

The woman proceeded to tell the entire roomful of patients about her upbringing. She was born and raised on a farm in Iowa, she said, and her aunts and uncles all had adjoining farms.

"My mother always had the whole tribe in for Sunday dinners once a month," the woman beamed. "Why, we'd all sit at these huge tables my father set up—my aunts and uncles and cousins and—*oh, my God!*" she exclaimed. I was astonished by the energy of her outburst.

"What's the matter?" I asked.

"Why, I just remembered—there was a Sunday or two when I had to take my Uncle Ed's head out of the mashed potatoes!"

Well, the room fairly exploded with laughter, but my friend was not to be the butt of that discovery. She blurted out, "But my uncle was no alcoholic!"

"Why not?" I asked. And then came the payoff for that lady. She pulled herself very erect in her chair and announced quite primly, "Because my mother didn't *allow* any alcoholics in the house!"

So there you have it. That woman didn't have an alcoholic relative because her mother wouldn't allow it! This is the point. Families protect such secrets through the generations. Yours may have done the same thing. There might have been aunts, uncles, grandparents, even older brothers or sisters who were full-blown alcoholics, but the family covered it up. It doesn't seem possible, but it happens all the time. This is the old skeleton-in-the-family-closet routine, and we've all been the victims of it! This is why an open and honest look into your own family tree is so important. The further back you go, the more obscure it will be, and you may have to settle for remembrances of events at which a relative displayed alcoholic behavior.

Many times a family will simply acknowledge that so-and-so was a "heavy drinker," or maybe he or she had a "drinking problem." This disclosure is usually followed by a remark such as, "I seem to remember Grandma talking about it, but it was all pretty hush-hush!"

If you are the parents of adopted children, you will probably want to recheck records given to you or available to you under the new disclosure regulations. Studies have been done on identical twins with alcoholic parents and identical twins adopted by alcoholic or at least heavy-drinking parents. In each case the twins of the natural alcoholic parents became alcoholic themselves, while the adopted twins, even though living with active alcoholics, showed little or no tendency toward alcoholism or alcohol abuse.

There can be no denying the genetic link to this disease. The *denial* usually comes in strong measure from you, the parent, in an understandable but foolish attempt to protect some family image. It is time for you to take off the mask and put on the gloves to do battle with the bottle! Hiding things under the proverbial rug is only going to hinder your understanding of, and treatment for, the disease.

Throughout this book we will talk about the importance of honesty in treating the disease of alcoholism. This means not pulling any punches with family members. It means being willing to examine all the possible avenues to success-ful treatment of the problem.

If a mother or a father is going to hide some important fact from the rest of the family, then there is not much hope for putting the family problem to rest.

You can trust the disease concept of alcoholism without its being a threat to whatever prideful image might be prevalent in the family. How often have you known or seen people go through years or maybe just months of a painful marriage because "there's never been a divorce" in the family? This kind of stiff-upper-lip attitude can only hinder your success as parents searching for methods to handle this disease.

Later on in this book we will examine your own drinking habits and what effects they may be having on the family unit. In the meantime, be comfortable with the disease concept; accept the possibility that what you are experiencing is the result of perhaps generations of alcohol abuse, and that genetics have played an important role in your present situation. We can't change what is already there, but we can change how you feel, think, and act about alcoholism; how *you*, as parents, put *your* shoulders to the wheel and begin doing something about the things you can change!

4
• • •
How Did
It Happen to
My Kid?

How *did* it happen to your kid?

Good question. In the last chapter we looked at genetically transmitted alcoholism. In this chapter, we'll look at some other reasons that may have played an important role in the development of the disease in your child.

We have been made aware in recent years of the *fetal alcohol syndrome,* the third most common birth defect involving mental retardation, and, for now, the only one that can be prevented. This syndrome affects babies born to women who are heavy drinkers, especially if the heavy drinking occurs during the first three months of pregnancy. These are the formative months when all of the baby's major body systems are being developed. When a mother is drinking, the alcohol invades the placenta and quickly enters the bloodstream and body tissues of the fetus. In essence, when pregnant mom drinks, so does unborn baby.

Mothers who are classified as "heavy drinkers"—those who consume perhaps six drinks a day—stand the greatest risk of bearing a child with fetal alcohol syndrome. Signs of the syndrome include low birth weight; small head size; some heart defects; arm, leg, and joint abnormalities; and perhaps mental retardation.

Dr. Donald W. Goodwin, a professor and chairman of psychiatry at the University of Kansas School of Medicine in Kansas City, believes "It's conceivable that maternal drinking during pregnancy produces a latent form of the fetal alcohol syndrome, and then becomes 'alcoholismic' as the adolescent discovers he can self-treat his hyperactivity with alcohol and get a calming effect."

Other experts in the field, who have studied children with fetal alcohol syndrome for many years, find that these children suffer from a wide range of alcohol-related abnormalities: everything from the full-blown syndrome with its facial abnormalities and central nervous system damage, small stature, etc., to those children who display normal social inhibitions, behavior problems, difficult or poor speech, hyperactivity, and yet in all other aspects appear physically normal.

Some of the other patterns of family alcoholism: college-age sons of alcoholics have a greater tolerance for alcohol than a studied control group of subjects, even though these sons haven't yet reached an age where they begin to drink heavily. Daughters of alcoholic mothers stand significantly greater risk of being alcoholic than if the father was the alcoholic parent; if *both* parents are alcoholic, the daughter faces a 400 percent greater risk of having the disease. Dr. Goodwin's studies have shown that sons of alcoholics are four to five times more likely to become alcoholic than sons of nonalcoholics.

We could go on and on, citing study after study in support of the *physical evidence* of the transmission of the disease, whether genetically or via intrauterine exposure. But there are also certain *psychological* factors at work in the development of alcoholism in your youngster.

Eminent psychiatrist Dr. Stanley Gitlow, a very knowledg-
able person in the alcohol treatment field, talks about the
"three Ds" that one looks for in the alcoholic: Depression,
Dependency, and Denial. My colleague at Gateway Treatment Center, John Mullan, lectures on a similar formula:
"Addiction plus Anxiety equals Compulsion."

Both of these, the "three Ds" and the "A-A-C" equation,
point up the need to pay attention to factors *other* than
purely genetic and physical addiction to alcohol. I have
heard my outstanding therapist-partner Paul Staley tell
many groups of patients in lectures that "There is a dual dependency to be treated with the alcoholic: one is physical,
and the other is psychological. These two," Paul continues,
"seem to build a parallel spiral."

Psychological dependency becomes a problem when the
drinker uses alcohol as a means to cope with everyday life.
Since alcohol sedates the central nervous system, the
alcoholic believes that his stress and anxiety will disap-
pear—the more he drinks, the fewer anxieties he has to
deal with. Unfortunately, this "release" is only temporary
and when the effects of the alcohol wear off, reality comes
flooding back. Back to the bottle. It's a vicious circle.

I say to my patients, "You thought you were using alcohol
as a means of coping. It's not until you have given up the
booze that you *really* begin to cope, probably for the first
time since you started steady, progressive drinking."

"We can't do anything about the addiction for the chemical (alcohol) if you are genetically predisposed," says John
Mullan. "All we can do is treat the part of the equation that
is available to us—the anxiety—in the hopes that we help
the alcoholic break the dependence on the drug and the
compulsion to continue using it until only oblivion is in
sight."

Who is the typical alcoholic? There's no such definition,
just as there is no "typical" diabetic. Alcoholism can strike
anyone, regardless of sex, race, occupation, or wealth. In
the words of Dr. Mansell Pattison, chairman of the Medical
College of Georgia, "There just isn't a personality common

to *all* alcoholics. There is no single alcoholic personality; but many alcoholics look distressingly the same!"

So we have to look at *types* of alcoholics. We are essentially dealing with three types of alcoholics, according to Dr. Arthur Knauert, whose work I find exciting. First, there is the *reactive alcoholic*. Dr. Knauert believes it is possible for anyone to become alcoholic if he or she is suddenly faced with an overwhelming emotional trauma that forces his or her coping mechanisms to break down or fail.

A good example is the sudden death of a family member. Such an event can cause an overwhelming emotional trauma that might limit the ability of the reactive personality to cope. This often leads to continuous drinking— drinking in order to cope—on a very dangerous level.

The *secondary alcoholic* is using alcohol in order to mask some underlying, deep-seated psychological problem. Therefore, it becomes difficult to accurately diagnose what problem the alcohol is hiding. When the alcoholic becomes alcohol-free, it is inevitable that his psychological problem will no longer be hidden, and will become treatable. Dr. Knauert believes that perhaps 40 percent of the people seeking treatment for alcoholism fall into the category of secondary alcoholics. If so, you can see that the psychological aspect of this disease plays a very important role in treatment, and enforces the idea that entire families must undergo treatment in order to help the alcoholic to recover.

The third type of alcoholic is the *primary alcoholic*. This person *loves* to drink, and relates to alcohol as if it were the perfect companion. The alcoholic finds constant, reliable comfort in drinking. Statistics show us that 50 percent of the parents of primary alcoholics are alcoholics themselves. Children of alcoholic parents are not absolutely predetermined to become alcoholics themselves. The odds are heavily stacked against them, however, and certain factors will increase or diminish the likelihood of alcoholism appearing in the child.

We know, for example, that kids from higher economic walks of life, where there is alcoholism in the home, suffer more from depression than their counterparts in the lower-income brackets. The high-bracket kids are expected to achieve more and conform more than their poorer counterparts, and thus feel greater stress and anxiety.

If the child in an alcoholic family is an only child, then he or she "goes it alone" with all the heartache, tears, anger, shame, and denial of having an alcoholic parent. This child grows up confused, depressed, and likely to have difficulty dealing with the opposite sex.

So you see, there are innumerable psychological factors that come into play in the development of alcoholism. No single factor is responsible; the blame is shared by both the physical and psychological sides of the makeup of human beings.

A few years ago, Dr. Stephanie Brown of the Stanford Medical Center Alcohol Clinic was quoted as saying, "There's an entire population of children who grew up looking so good, acting so perfect, achieving so much. Then, in their 20s and 30s, things begin to fall apart—more than half of them will turn to alcohol and perpetuate the problem from generation to generation."

Brown was referring to the seemingly well-adjusted, over-achieving youngsters that we have all known and loved in our own lives. She points out that misbehaving, troublesome youngsters—the ones who are thought to have a 50 to 60 percent risk of following an alcoholic parent into the disease—are not the only targets of "John Barleycorn."

Highly regarded author Dr. Claudia Black is a true expert in the treatment of the children of alcoholic parents. Claudia has said many times in her workshops, "The model 6-year-old I see in my office today will, without treatment, become the struggling, depressed, soon-to-be-alcoholic 35-year-old I saw yesterday."

It is essential that you, the parent, closely examine your *own* drinking background, the current state of your drinking, and where a genetic transmission of the disease may have occurred. You can't change whatever it was that led your son or daughter to drink, but you can move ahead, and begin to understand how to help your alcoholic or alcohol-abusing youngster to handle his or her life.

There are so many variables and symptoms that we use to help identify an alcoholic. You can find list after list of pertinent questions that can be asked, such as:

- Do you drink in the morning?
- Do you avoid functions where you know alcohol won't be served?
- Have you had a blackout? (The inability to recall what happened during drinking, even though certain tasks were completed; e.g., driving home: "I obviously *got* home, but *how?*" "I *started out* with Jeannie, but who did I end up with?" "Where did this check come from?" "Who did I agree to meet for a job interview?", etc.)
- What's happening to your friendships because of your drinking?
- Is your job (college work, high school classes) affected by your drinking?
- Are you in trouble with the law?
- How *much* are you drinking?
- Are you having a hard time stopping after one or two?
- What are you doing to obtain alcohol?
- Are you aware of your altered state of behavior when you are drinking?
- What's happening in your relationships with your family?

This book will show you how *not* to take on unwarranted responsibility, guilt, and behaviors that have left you frustrated, heartsick, and emotionally at a standstill in learning how to deal with your alcoholic young person. It will show you how to get on with your life without the haunting fear of facing another day, week, month, or series of years with alcoholism in your family.

If you are a drinking parent or if you know of alcoholism in your family background, you need search no further for the reasons that the disease has stricken your child. If there are no traceable or visible signs of family alcoholism, and yet it is quite apparent that your young person is in trouble with alcohol, then you must be prepared to examine your own behavior as well as that of the abusing young person, in order to seek answers to the question of why he or she is turning to a chemical substance as a means of attempting to cope with life's problems. Let's move forward together, then, with courage and with an eagerness to learn from the experiences of others, and from our own abilities to use new tools for family recovery!

5
• • •
Mom and Dad: Classic Enablers

"I thought I was helping Sally when I called in sick for her!"

"He kept saying to me, 'Dad, just give me one more little loan, and I'll make it for sure this time!' Hell, I thought I was doing the kid a favor!"

Sound familiar? It should, because phrases like these are heard daily, emanating from the mouths of parents who are asking themselves, "What went wrong?" and "Where did we make the mistakes?" The truth is, parents are the classic *enablers*, people who prevent other people from realizing the consequences of their actions by covering up. The enabler always picks up the pieces after the damage has been done.

"What's wrong with that?" you may ask. "What are parents for except to help their children?" All kinds of excuses may be called up to make a solid argument for enabling. The problem is that you probably are confusing *helping* with *enabling*. It's one thing to stop and help someone in trouble, say, to change a tire. But would you tell

34

the stranded stranger, "Why don't you just go on and do some shopping? *I'll* change the tire for you!" That would be pretty silly, wouldn't it? *You* already know how to change a tire, but maybe the person you are trying to help needs to learn how to do the job. By performing the function for him or her, you are enabling the person to avoid accepting any responsibility for learning how to change a tire. He or she will be programmed to think, "I never have to learn how to do that! Someone can always do it for me!"

It works the same way when parents continue to pile the responsibilities for their offsprings' actions on their own shoulders. What mother reading this can honestly say she would have learned how to bake a delicious pie or manage a complex household or a business if everyone had done the jobs for her?

What father reading this can ever forget the impatience of first learning to drive? Maybe you were fortunate enough to have had some formal driving education classes, but chances are your father or grandfather taught you how to drive. You probably remember saying in a familiar little-boy whine, "Aw, c'mon, Dad, let *me* do it!"

The very successful advertising campaign of a few years ago that said, "You've come a long way, baby!" is another good example of how we constantly strive to *do things for ourselves*. What is it, then, that makes us as parents forget all the learning experiences we were forced to undertake, and take over total responsibility for the young adults in our household? It's *guilt!*

We are constantly seeking ways to make life easier for our children, to make it better than it was for us, even if our lives were filled with nothing but servants and Rolls Royces. Of course, parents are quick to accept guilt and blame for the actions of an alcoholic youngster, even more so than with many other diseases that can strike a family.

Many examples of typical parental enabling involving a chemically dependent young person come to mind. Mr. and Mrs. Smedley, for instance, wanted to buy a car for their daughter. They not only gave her the downpayment, but

Dad was also perfectly willing to cosign her installment loan at the bank. Daughter Ginny was supposed to make the payments herself; she had a good-paying job and had a fairly workable budget to help provide for her monthly rent, food, entertainment, and all the other necessities.

But Ginny had a drinking problem, a problem that was growing more pronounced. She began, frankly, to exhibit the signs of full-blown alcoholism. She was starting her drinking episodes earlier and earlier in the week. The Friday night social hour was now beginning to start, at least for Ginny, at three in the afternoon. She had a job with an insurance agency, and time off was not a very big problem. When her boss was out of the office on a business trip, a rather frequent happening, Ginny could shut down his office early without disrupting the flow of things.

She began to meet her friends at the local watering holes well before the legitimate "happy hour" was scheduled to begin at 4:30 or 5:00. Her friends, for the most part, had jobs that did not call for regular daily hours. Two of them were flight attendants with many days off at a stretch. One friend was in business for herself, and another was unemployed for great stretches of time. Her time was never a problem, and she was always ready to party.

As Ginny's drinking became more pronounced and more dangerous, the surefire signs of irresponsibility clearly became a part of her life. The monthly rent on her apartment was sometimes a few days overdue; often it was a week late. Her refrigerator never seemed to contain much nutritious food, leaving more and more room for bottles of wine and cans of beer. The beer, her mother noticed, was an expensive brand, and the wine was growing from fifths to either half-liters or those fancy cartons that contain built-in pouring spouts.

Ginny first got into trouble with her car payments when she had a particularly heavy weekend of partying and suffered her first recognizable case of alcoholic amnesia—*blackouts*, as they are called. Ginny sat down on Monday afternoon and glanced at her checkbook. There were two checks missing, and her check register failed to provide any clue.

For a time Ginny was hard-pressed to remember what checks she had written over the weekend. Then it came to her. "I made my car payment!" she thought. "I just forgot to enter it in my checkbook." OK; so far, so good. Anyone can make a "dumb" mistake like that. We've all been guilty of the same kinds of things ourselves. But this accounting for the car payment didn't solve the mystery of the other missing check. To whom was that one written and for how much?

She racked her brain, but for the life of her she could not remember where she might have written that check. Late on Monday it came to her. Ginny began to review where she had stopped after work on Friday. She had had a few friends over for a football-watching party on Sunday, and she hated Saturday shopping. So, Ginny reasoned, she would have stopped at the grocery store on Friday on her way home from work and gotten all the things she needed for Sunday.

So far, so good. She looked in her checkbook register and, sure enough, there was the entry and the amount. But still there was a missing sum and a missing check. Then she recalled having also stopped at the liquor store for more supplies. That must have been it. Still, Ginny couldn't remember the amount of the check she may have written, and she had no receipt from the liquor store. It had probably been thrown out along with the trash.

In order ·to reconcile her checkbook, Ginny overestimated the amount she may have written at the liquor store and seemed comfortable enough to be back on track with her funds.

Fifteen days after this checkbook-accounting episode, Ginny arrived home to find a delinquency notice from the bank. Her car payment had not been received. Ginny was angry at first. "Damn bank!" she muttered as she crumpled up the delinquency notice and pitched it. "Computers are the bane of my existence. I mailed my payment on time!"

Dad Smedley, as the cosigner of the note for Ginny's car, also received the delinquency notice. He phoned Ginny to ask what was going on.

"It's nothing, Dad. The bank screwed up. I made that payment when I paid my other bills. I know I did because it was missing from my checkbook accounting and it took me some time to find out that I had forgotten to enter the amount. Not to worry!"

Dad didn't worry. After all, Ginny was a responsible girl, and if she said she had made the payment, then she had. Matter closed.

But the matter *wasn't* closed. Six days later, a second delinquency notice arrived: one for Ginny and one more for Dad. This time, Dad wanted more of an explanation.

"Look at your payment book, Ginny. You would have recorded your check number and the date in there, wouldn't you?"

After all, that's what he did, didn't he? Well, Ginny saw no reason to tell her dad she *never* did that; it took too much time and she'd never needed that information before. What she could do, she told her dad, is phone the bank right away and tell them when she had made the payment. Dad told her to get back to him.

"I don't like having these delinquency notices on *my* records, Ginny!"

Ginny assured Dad Smedley that she would call him right back as soon as she had proven her point to the bank. Ginny grabbed her payment book for support in informing the bank that she always made her payments at the same time every month. Perhaps she'd have to read them the dates of her payments from her checkbook, and in that checkbook she *did* follow the practice of noting which car payment number the check represented.

As Ginny opened her payment book, the missing payment coupon fluttered to the floor. She had apparently never mailed the coupon or the check. She knew now that her dad was going to be angry—and, even worse, what had become of the missing check? To whom was it written? For how much? She had been so sure that it was the car payment.

Ginny learned to her dismay that she had written a second check to another liquor store on Saturday when she worried about not having a big enough supply for her party. She then recalled that she had asked permission to write her check for fifty extra dollars.

Ginny's drinking bout over the weekend had produced a blackout. She had remembered neither the facts about her unpaid car payment, which she was *positive* she had made, nor could account for the extra cash received from the liquor store check.

Here's the enabling sequence. Dad Smedley listened with some patience to the "cock and bull" story Ginny concocted to cover the car payment incident. She now didn't have the funds to make the payment. Could Dad do it, just once? Of course, he could! After all, Ginny was a favorite daughter. Dad didn't know at the time about the drinking episode. It *did* bother Ginny, however, and she confided to her mother that she believed she had done too much partying the previous weekend and really didn't know what had happened to the money for the car payment. She had just overspent as far as she was concerned. It wouldn't happen again, she assured her mother.

Ginny's drinking grew worse. Her drinking episodes became longer and stronger as the disease progressed. Soon, it was a regular occurrence that every month or so Dad and Mom Smedley were making one payment or another for Ginny. Mostly it was the car. She loved that car; it was her pride and joy. The Smedleys talked openly of not bailing Ginny out anymore with the bank, but it was an idle threat. Ginny pleaded each time, blaming her partying or "a friend who needed help" for her lack of sufficient funds to cover her payments.

The parents, instead of helping Ginny as they thought they were, instead of coming to her aid while she was in trouble, were caught in a web of massive enabling. They were excusing her alcohol abuse and its resulting behavior patterns as a temporary thing. By continuing to bail their daughter out of her financial difficulties, they were, in essence, rewarding her. She was not being forced to confront the consequences of her alcoholic behavior.

In group therapy, when the Smedleys were confronted by other members about their continuing to make her payments, the Smedleys replied, "But it's so hard to turn Ginny down. And we're certain she's cutting down on her drinking!" Dad Smedley even reinforced how important the car was to Ginny and said that, if it were to go "down the tubes" because of "one or two payments," Ginny would be "devastated," perhaps even causing her to drink more.

So the enabling monster had struck the Smedleys. They continued to cover for Ginny's growing financial irresponsibility. When she finally lost her job and was forced to move from her apartment they took her back home. Not in one instance did they confront Ginny with the fact that her full-blown alcoholism was causing her problems. They weren't *helping* their daughter; they were *enabling*.

When the Smedley family sought treatment as a family for the alcoholism, the enabling stopped. Ginny learned that Mom and Dad were responsible neither for her drinking nor for her incurred debts. Mom and Dad learned that all they had been doing, out of misplaced parental love, was enabling Ginny not to face her alcohol problem. It was a hard lesson for everyone involved, but Ginny finally lost her prized car. The Smedleys, through therapy, got well enough to say "no more." They stopped enabling.

The concept that may be difficult for you as a parent to understand is that you must stop enabling because you *do* love your children. You love them so much, in fact, that you must stop protecting them from their own behavior. I have heard young adults literally scream at a parent, "If you *loved* me, you'd do it!" That's pretty heavy stuff to lay on parents who are already suffering from a large dose of guilt. "If you loved me" covers too many sins, and you, as parents, need to be prepared to counter such statements with, "It's *because* we love you that we aren't going to do this [whatever] for you anymore!"

It's important never to use a hard-line approach as a threat either to force the person to seek help or as an excuse to turn back to enabling. For example, stay away from this sort of ultimatum: "I'll make your car payment one more time, but only if you get some help for your drinking!" or "Let's see if you stay off the booze first; *then* I'll look at making some payments for you." This is like telling a person to get his or her cancer under control and *then* you'll help the person get to a doctor.

The alcohol-abusing young person needs help for the alcohol problem. Don't reward the youngster for seeking help by going back to enabling. It would be OK for parents to pay for treatment, for example. However, the patient should be encouraged to contribute to the family cost of such treatment. It would mean very little to the young person if Mom and Dad paid for the whole thing; it would be just like picking up the car payments, relieving the delinquent of all responsibility.

Many times, a young person in treatment can't afford to pay anything. Should Mom and Dad refuse help? Of course not. But they might make a loan of treatment money to the young person. By putting responsibility where it clearly belongs, you are helping the alcoholic or alcohol abuser face what his or her commitment is to getting well. As the classic enablers, Mom and Dad think that "one more time" is the right way to make a point. "I just know it'll work *this* time!" is the most pitiful excuse for preventing a youngster from facing the consequences of his or her own actions.

Money isn't the only way parents enable. Take the example of Brett, age twenty-three. Brett and his wife had been having marital difficulties. His drinking was also getting progressively worse. His wife, Maggie, told him that she could not tolerate his drinking and the "awful" things he said to her when he was out "with the boys" on Friday nights. She never knew how much of a paycheck he would have left. Maggie was pregnant for the first time. They had a nice, if small, home in a fairly young and affluent neighborhood.

Both Maggie and Brett had increased their drinking as a couple, but Maggie realized early in their marriage that she had a very low tolerance to alcohol, and she quit drinking almost totally. Brett's drinking continued to get more severe. Brett's parents, Lou and Marsha Phillips, "adored" their daughter-in-law and were anxiously awaiting the birth of their first grandchild.

After the last really hard drinking episode that Brett went through he came home to find Maggie in tears, with his best suitcase packed and sitting in the hallway. Brett was furious when Maggie told him, "I don't care where you go, but you can't stay here. I've had it with your drinking, and until you go for help, you can't live with me!"

Needless to say, Lou and Marsha were heartbroken. How could their daughter-in-law be so heartless? This wasn't the same Maggie they had known in the past. Lou was hearing Marsha refer to Maggie as "bitchy" and as "a spoiled brat." And where was Brett to live? He certainly couldn't afford an apartment; they barely made it as it was. Lou and Marsha could think of only one thing. Brett moved back home, back to his old room, just as if he had never married and left home in the first place.

The alcohol problem was discussed, certainly, but Lou and Marsha could not face up to the possibility that their son might be alcoholic. They knew there was plenty of alcoholism in the family, on both sides. Yet they were certain that Brett's problems were being caused by the pressures of pending fatherhood. Maggie became the heavy in the drama, and, as she told it, "I almost was convinced myself that it was really my fault, that *I* might *really* be the cause of Brett's alcoholism!"

The Phillipses were a "family" once again, just like in the "old days" before Brett had gone off to college and then come home with a new bride. Marsha Phillips began to do more and more enabling. She cooked meals for Brett, ironed his shirts, and even packed his lunch. Each and every Friday night Brett met his gang of guys just as if nothing had changed. Brett drank, got drunk, and was allowed to come home at any time he desired.

Once or twice Lou Phillips asked his son if he "wasn't out a little late last night." That's as far as it generally went. Marsha would butt in with, "Lou, after all, Brett's not a baby anymore!" But Marsha continued to treat him that way, just like a baby—*her* baby.

Maggie tried in vain to persuade Lou and Marsha to stop helping Brett run away from his responsibilities, both to her and to their unborn child as well as to himself. She didn't know the term *enabler* then, but she had the right idea.

"You just can't keep him from looking at his own problems anymore!" she would cry in frustration. But Marsha remained locked into the pattern of wanting to pick up the pieces. Her family nest was filled again with her son at home, and she was willing to do anything to keep it that way.

Lou continued to support his wife's actions. He didn't want to upset Marsha, so he enabled Marsha to continue protecting Brett.

Brett didn't change. He didn't have to. Mom and Dad had made it unnecessary for Brett to face up to his alcoholism. Since they, the parents, were providing him with all the comforts of home, *his* home, he didn't find it necessary to return to Maggie or make any efforts at reconciliation by seeking help for his drinking.

Maggie sought help in therapy, and to her credit, got stronger. She got well enough to file for divorce from Brett.

The parents sought help for "their kids," and in so doing they were confronted with how all-encompassing their enabling practices had been. After many tearful therapy sessions Lou and Marsha agreed to kick their son out of their house in the hope that it might help him realize the seriousness of his situation.

Brett and Maggie entered family treatment together, even though she did not remove the threat of the divorce right away. Lou and Marsha also got help for themselves and began to see how they had confused helping with enabling. They began to learn that they had used their love for their son as a weapon for his destruction as opposed to his recovery. There have been some one-day drinking episodes since the couple entered treatment. But Brett is no longer allowed to come home to his parent's house. If there is difficulty between Brett and Maggie, the parents will no longer provide a haven for Brett. They will, at the drop of a hat, take their new grandson for a night or two, to give Maggie and Brett a chance to work out their problems by themselves or with their therapist.

The biggest change has occurred in Marsha. She has a new awareness of herself as someone who can help with understanding instead of interfering as an enabler. She is still willing to open her home and her heart to both Brett and Maggie on a new, realistic level. She is becoming aware of how much she and her husband Lou contributed to the delay in getting Brett on the road to facing his problem.

What is most significant in this story is the revelation of just how much Marsha had been denying the drinking problem. It was as if her own family background of alcoholism had reared up from the grave and was making an attempt to resurrect itself. She and Lou had tried so valiantly to turn away from the obviousness of the situation that they just contributed to new problems for themselves.

The idea of their grandchild being born into a home with no father had been just enough motivation to get Lou and Marsha to take some action. When Maggie filed for divorce and accused them of contributing to the problem, when all the time they thought they had been helping, it turned the tide. As a family unit all four persons can openly talk of Marsha's alcoholic mother and Lou's alcoholic grandfather.

Instead of hiding the family ghosts, the Phillipses, young and old, have bent over backward to stop being enablers. When either parent feels that something he or she might do will prevent responsibility on the part of their son they put the idea up to each other for thorough discussion. Even better is the idea that grew from family therapy: they put the idea or plan squarely before Brett and Maggie, asking, "What are your feelings about this?"

Lou has been particularly pleased to see his son turn down some help from him because he would rather do it himself. It is a sign of growing on the part of each family member. It was growth that was needed and was a long time coming!

As a parent, ask yourself what particular things you may be doing under the guise of love. Are you denying an obvious drinking problem with a son or daughter so strongly that you are resorting to enabling at every turn to prevent positive action?

Be honest with yourself and ask how much this denial of the problem is really preventing a get-well situation. The more you, the parents, say, "Well, he'll grow out of this" or "*All* the college kids are drinking too much these days," the more you hide under the cover of denial. It may be excruciatingly painful for you to admit that a drinking problem *does* exist. Far better to face the reality of the situation than to continue to enable the problem.

ENABLING QUESTIONNAIRE

Here's a checklist for you to use in trying to determine what I call your *enabling ability,* or EA. Be honest in giving your answers to these questions, and be sure that *each* of you answers each question (only one of you may have to answer "yes" to a particular question, but this will still have a significant effect on your alcoholic son or daughter). You parents will be the winners; every tool you learn to master will help you deal with and live with the reality of an alcoholic youngster in your life.

1. Do we purposely intervene in a family argument our child may be having with his or her spouse over drinking?

2. Have we or do we now provide certain "safe harbors" for our child when he or she is in difficulty as the result of the use of alcohol?
3. Have we truly examined our own drinking habits and then excused our children's drinking or abuse because of what we have done?
4. Have we avoided openly talking about family alcoholism—with the result that our children don't know that they might have inherited the genetic predisposition to drink?
5. Are we inclined to keep loaning money even though we suspect the money is not being used for the requested purpose but is going toward drinking?
6. Have we intervened in matters of the law, hiring the best lawyer available when our youngster gets into police trouble because of drinking?
7. Have we not truly made thinking about what to do with this drinking problem a priority, assuming it will "go away"?
8. Have we been excusing an obvious problem because it seems that "everyone else" has the same problem?
9. Have we let our own guilt carry us so far that we are afraid we might lose the love of our child if we refuse to comply with his or her requests, even though we know we shouldn't give in?
10. Do we find ourselves searching around for some plausible reason why we might have a young person with an alcohol problem instead of asking ourselves, "What can we do about the problem?"

In your individual case certain of the questions above may carry more weight than others, so you will have to judge for yourself how strong your EA truly is. Suffice it to say, however, that the more "yes" answers you gave to these questions, the higher and more dangerous your enabling ability is. Essentially, these questions and answers should make you think about what you as parents have probably been doing for a long time, enabling like pros, so you can see where you need to make some changes.

Don't be afraid to get back into the habit of saying "no." It has a lot of value, no matter how strong the pain the first time you say it. Saying "no" to someone you love with an alcohol problem also helps you say "yes": "No, I won't continue to be a part of your continued drinking problem, but *yes*, I stand ready to help you be a part of the family again when *you* make the decision to seek help!"

It's a good feeling to stop enabling and start helping in positive ways. Try it!

6

• • •

The Guilt
Trip

Parents ask themselves these questions over and over:
"What have we done?"
"Why is this happening to us?"
"Is God punishing us for something?"
Perfectly natural. You are a parent, and you feel an
enormous sense of responsibility for that living creature
you have helped bring into the world. But there is a vast dif-
ference between feeling *responsible* and feeling *guilty*.

All parents go through the same feelings of shame, guilt,
anger, and denial that the alcoholic experiences. This is the
primary reason for having parents participate in treatment
along with the alcoholic: to give everyone a chance to deal
with those emotions. You see, all members of the family
have gotten sick together, and all members of the family
need to get well together!

It is time for you to remove the "sackcloth and ashes"
that you have been draping conveniently over your

shoulders. It's been your way of accepting guilt and not just common, everyday responsibility! This is a guilt that fairly screams at you every time your alcohol-abusing youngster gets into a jam. In order to help you look at what you've been doing, think about what was said in Chapter 2 about the disease concept of alcoholism.

Knowing that the disease is genetically transmitted from generation to generation, it only stands to reason that you feel a great sense of guilt for having been one of the links that forged that disease chain. Well, you can forget that guilt! You had no more control over passing that disease along to your child than you had control over the other genetic factors such as eye or hair color. The predisposition to alcoholism was just one other genetic factor that went into the physical and psychological components of the mind and body of the child you helped bring into the world.

What you do have instead of guilt is a responsibility to inform your offspring of their potential for having the disease of alcoholism. But that's where it ends for you as a parent, and you really have to believe that if you are going to get well yourself. Once informed, it's up to the young person to make up his or her mind about how far to push that potential toward actuality.

It's like looking at a loaded revolver on the firing range table. You can point out the bullets in the chamber; the chances of the gun discharging if one pulls the trigger are very high. Having pointed out the potential, you have acted in a responsible manner. If someone then picks up that loaded revolver and, having heard all the facts about its potential for danger, pulls the trigger and discharges a bullet or two, that is *not* your responsibility!

This feeling of wanting to accept guilt for everything is a longstanding pattern for parents. Just think back to your own childhood and some of the times you were made to feel guilty over a particular incident. Suppose you were playing ball in your living room, something your mother had repeatedly told you not to do. The ball hit a favorite vase and broke it.

"Why, oh, *why* didn't you listen to me?" your mother wailed. She may then have followed up with a real guilt clincher:

"That was my *favorite* thing in the whole house! It's been in my family for years!"

Well! The guilt button was already waiting to be pushed because you were told from the very first not to play ball in the living room. When Mother nailed you about the "favorite thing" the guilt was firmly embedded. From then on you may have found it very easy to accept guilt for things your brothers or sisters or even playmates did (while in your house), trying to make up for the incident that "caused Mom so much pain."

You had a *responsibility* not to play ball in the living room, knowing the consequences. You did not have to accept guilt that the item you broke was Mother's *favorite* thing; that was her definition and might have applied to any object that you had broken with the ball, since she had told you not to play ball in the living room in the first place.

In the particular case of alcohol abuse it becomes very easy for you, the parent, to wonder what it was that *you* did to cause your child to abuse the substance. Is there something that you overlooked in teaching him or her values and morals? Maybe you should have gone to Sunday school, church, or temple more often.

You grasp at all the straws available; should you have made more effort to participate in the Boy Scouts, Campfire Girls, PTA, 4-H, or what have you? The list of speculations is endless. If you so desire, you can find more reasons for accepting the blame than items in the current Sears catalogue!

The key here is to remember that when you accept the guilt, putting it all on your shoulders, you deprive the young person of the chance to realize the consequences of his or her own alcoholic behavior. And why *should* your child have to feel guilty about a particular action if you are around to take the blame?

If the alcohol abuser wrecks the family car's fender by

hitting the side of the garage trying to park after an evening of boozing it up, whose fault is it? If you're a blame-taking parent, you can rush right into junior's arms and tell him, "Don't worry, honey! *I* should have cleaned out the garage so it was easier for you to park without hitting something."

Not a word about "honey" being sloshed to the gills and probably unable to maneuver the family bus even if the garage was stark naked of any other objects; just you the parent rushing in to the rescue again! How many times it becomes convenient to pick up the pieces of a child's life by taking the blame for his own actions!

"I just don't know *how* I'll pay this month's rent!" Well, *we* know who will pay, don't we? Good old Dad or Mom, particularly if the "guilt button" is on and operating. What makes it impossible for you to confront the abuser? Isn't it important for you to know where the money for the rent has gone? Or is it just possible that you do know and are afraid of hearing the answer?

This kind of covering up goes on day in and day out for many weeks, months, or even years. It all happens because the parents feel a deep sense of guilt about why their young person is spending the rent money on booze. The guilt is often expressed as, "He [she] drinks too much because I've been too hard on him [her] when he [she] was growing up!" Still taking the blame for breaking Mom's favorite vase? What utter nonsense! "Honey" is drinking too much be-cause of many different factors, including the possibility of an inherited genetic disability that you had no control over. Stop making excuses for him or her and get to the nitty-gritty of the problem: you must learn, in short, to confront!

What makes confronting so difficult, anyhow? You have done a lot of it in the process of rearing your kids. How many times have you found yourself saying, "OK, which one of you did it?" or "Nobody leaves this house until I get an explanation for why the chores weren't done!"?

See? You have been a confronter all your born days. It's only when a taboo subject like drinking comes to mind that you turn to a mass of jelly. That's simply not acceptable. It becomes absolutely essential that you find the courage to say, "We need to talk about your drinking."

The longer you put off the confrontation, the more you allow yourself to ride the guilt trip to its ultimate conclusion, the one that makes you believe you really *are* responsible for the alcoholic behavior you are witnessing.

Let's look at three things that guilt makes you do, stifling the family's efforts ever to get well:

1. Guilt constantly involves you in the enabling process, preventing you from helping your youngster get well.
2. Guilt cements you in a permanent position, firmly nailed to the cross. It never lets you climb down off that cross. It makes you continue to accept the punishment that you believe you deserve.
3. Guilt keeps you from ever disclosing the possible source of the family's alcoholism. That's unfair! Your kids have every right to know where the genetic deficiency came from in the first place.

A good example of a parent's using guilt to hinder the get-well process for a child is the case involving Sharon.

Sharon had been in and out of trouble and in and out of treatment a number of times. Her parents entered treatment to get well for themselves during one period when Sharon was still actively involved in treatment. Sharon began to have periodic relapses. She would drink for an evening, be remorseful, and go back into treatment. Her parents held up very well, not doing much of anything except commending and complimenting their daughter when she would reenter her treatment, make regular contact with her therapist, and have good attendance at her group sessions.

Then Sharon decided to hit the road. She left the program, her parents' home, and the state. The parents turned from controlled composure to real fear for Sharon. After two weeks of not hearing from her, Sharon phoned. She had been on a drinking spree, was in another state, and was broke. She wanted to come home but had no money. The parents sent her money, with the firm promise from

Sharon that she would be on the next available plane and would be home, ready to reenter treatment.

Hours passed, then days. No Sharon. No phone calls, either. Her parents were frustrated and very angry! They felt they had been taken in and swore before their group that they would never again be a party to Sharon's trickery. After two more weeks it was obvious that Sharon had no intention of returning home. Her parents faithfully continued working in group. They said it would be a "cold day in hell" before they would send any more money.

Then worry set in. It had been much too long not to have heard from Sharon. She had never stayed out of touch with her family for so long. Sharon's mother became increasingly concerned. She began to talk of doing "anything" just to hear from Sharon. The parents' group urged both parents to have faith and remain strong.

Another three days passed before Sharon finally called—collect. She was "sober" now, she said, and really wanted to come home.

"We're not sending you another plane ticket to cash in," her stern father told her, "You'll have to find your own way home!"

Sharon's mother, listening on the extension, confirmed that both parents were in agreement; they would not send her any more money.

More agonizing time passed without an appearance or phone call from Sharon. As the days passed Sharon's mother became more frantic. She began to tell her group that "maybe she was too tough on Sharon." Sharon's father held to his resolve not to do any more, but it was soon obvious that massive guilt had overtaken her mother.

Mom changed her tune dramatically. "I sure won't send her money for an airplane ticket home, but I don't think it would hurt to send her a bus ticket," she told her group one night. "I'm really getting worried about where she is, or even if she's alive!"

The group tried to reason with the mother, attempting to show her that her own guilt was beginning to show *and* get in the way. But the guilt trip was already started, and the mother began to say things like, "Maybe we were too hard on Sharon when she called the first time and told us she had cashed in the plane ticket! I wonder if maybe we didn't frighten her."

When Sharon called, once again collect, her father was beginning to show some real anger. He told her that he would not allow anyone to accept any more collect calls from her and that she needed to find a way to come back home. Sharon's mother, however, caved in to her own guilt trip pressure. She told Sharon that if Sharon promised to come back home and return to her treatment program, she (mother) would loan Sharon money for a bus ticket home.

Needless to say, Sharon's father was dismayed and even angrier that his wife would make such an offer to Sharon, particularly since she did it without any prior consultation with her husband. Mother wired the bus money. Sharon came home, reentered her treatment for alcoholism, and stayed with it just long enough for everyone to breathe a collective sigh of relief. As soon as Sharon's mother was comfortable with what she had done (sent the bus ticket money) Sharon did the predictable: She took off again, without warning, and the whole process started anew.

Sharon's mother was furious—at Sharon, at her husband, at herself. She believed she had been taken in and freely admitted to her group that she had been "a damn fool" and that she had let her own guilt take charge of her better judgment.

"Never again!" she vowed solemnly. "I've learned my lesson; Sharon simply pushes my guilt button, and she gets anything she wants from me!"

Sharon stayed away from home and basically out of contact for more than three months. The longer she was away, the more the worry built up in Sharon's mother, but she was determined to stick to her guns. Even if Sharon begged to come home, her mother was not going to send her money.

Sharon moved back to the city where her parents lived. She did not ask for money and apparently was getting her means from a boyfriend. They lived together as part of a commune. For the better part of six months Sharon's parents neither sent her money nor supported her in any other way. On the very few occasions when they heard from her they could tell that she had been drinking. There was some indication that she had started using other drugs in addition to alcohol.

Sharon's mother slowly began to start herself along another guilt trip. The presence of other drugs in Sharon's life was the trigger for Sharon's mother. She began to say that maybe "this time Sharon was *ready* for help" and that she (mother) would be interested in helping her get back into treatment. The die was cast.

Sharon called a few days after her mother had once again expressed an interest in helping Sharon do something about getting her life in order. Sharon called from a pay phone. She told her mother that she had been "in some kind of trouble" and she needed fifty dollars to avoid going to jail. Her mother was torn with guilt. Had she caused all this unhappiness in her daughter's troubled life? She had three other children, and all of them were doing so well. It *must* be something that she was doing to Sharon, some element of nurturing that she had missed giving to Sharon.

But Sharon's father reasoned differently: Now was the time to straighten her out. "Let her spend five days in the slammer!" he said. "Maybe she'll finally understand the consequences of her alcoholic and drug life!"

The family held a conference. Should they give Sharon the fifty dollars? Every family member, including Sharon's mother, decided *not* to give her the jail fine money. This time Sharon was going to have to "tough it out." But once one sets out on the guilt path, it is very difficult to make a different turn. Sharon's mother reverted to form, although doing so in a way that could allow her to believe she was not contributing to the enabling process.

Sharon was to have a birthday. Mother sent her a check for fifty dollars with a birthday card that said, "Get something pretty for yourself!"

Sharon didn't do the slammer time.

Let's look at what Sharon's mother was doing. No, she certainly did not pay the jail fine for her daughter. She only gave her a birthday check to "buy something nice." We all know what Sharon would do, however. She would avoid going to jail at any cost, and Mother would avoid coming to grips with how far down the guilt path she had trod.

Sharon was no further along in her get-well program because she had been bailed out once again, only this time it was a more subtle maneuver. For Sharon's mother it was a long time before she could ever see how she was only enabling her daughter not to come to grips, once again, with her serious alcohol/drug problem. Guilt was the victor.

What can you do to avoid the same kind of trap? It would be foolhardy and senseless for me to suggest that you should feel good or secure about leaving your young person stranded as Sharon was. We hear too many horrendous stories of what happens with so-called runaways, and obviously you are not anxious to leave your youngster in an absolutely hopeless fix. So you can try an alternative.

If your youngster wants to have you send money, and you refuse, you can still provide a way home without being an enabler. Try this: "You're in trouble and need to come home. We'll get a prepaid airline (bus, train) ticket for you. You go to the airport (station) and a seat will be waiting for you."

This can really accomplish your purpose. You are not sending money to the young person so he or she can spend more on alcohol, but you are providing a way home. If he or she is serious about wanting to come home, then you are making it possible, but you are not enabling by providing funds for continued alcohol use.

Using this method, a number of young people have been coaxed back home and into treatment, either for the first time or to pick up their program where it was voluntarily interrupted.

As you see, there are alternatives to feeling quilty. Now let's look at some other tools that can help you get yourself off the guilt trip. Like all tools, these will do you some good only if you pick them up and use them. If you just let them lie there, you will continue in the same old ways, doing the same old enabling things because of your guilt.

PROMISES TO MAKE TO YOURSELF

1. I promise to begin getting well just for me, without regard to whether it meets anyone else's needs.
2. I promise to ask myself, "Is this a *helping* or an *enabling* action I am performing?"
3. I promise to understand that I am not personally responsible for whether or not my child is drinking.
4. I promise that I will try not to let my "buttons" be pushed by anger, either at myself or at me by others.
5. I promise I will act from a foundation of *love*, not pity, remorse, or personal revenge.

These promises can launch you on a new trip toward your own recovery. The last promise bears amplification and drilling on your part until it becomes second nature. How many times during your rearing of the children have you been wailed at with words something like "You'd do it if you *loved* me!" or "If you *really* loved me, you'd do this for me!"

Talk about pushing buttons! That one just hangs out there asking, pleading, *begging* to be pushed! It makes you respond with all the basic instincts that lie within parents. Love is so much a part of child rearing that it forms the beginning, middle, and end of your relationship with your children. You grow up in parenting constantly telling your children that you love them. Maybe you even have a bumper sticker on your car that asks, "Have you hugged your kid today?"

Everywhere you turn you are being bombarded with words, music, poetry, television, movies; the message is love! So what happens when you refuse to do something for your youngster? You are accused of not loving him or her enough! What you have to learn is that everything you do that appears to be punishment is actually an act of love. You must learn to say to the alcohol-abusing young person, "I am not giving you the money [or what have you] because I *do* love you! For me to give you this would only be hurting you, not helping you!"

This will be hard for you and for the young person. Your child will not understand how you can say you love him or her in one breath and then refuse to help in another. You too will find it difficult to reconcile those two things. But you must understand the reasoning.

If you refuse to do something you know is prompted by guilt, you are forcing the other person to turn to another resource, namely himself or herself. As long as you are always there to pick up the pieces, there is very little incentive for your child to confront himself or herself about the issue of alcohol abuse.

So make Promise 5 part of your everyday dealings with your alcohol-abusing young person. Don't let anyone push your guilt button!

Here are a couple of other ways to get off the guilt trip:

1. Look beyond the immediate act and project a little bit down the road. Is what you are doing today as an act of "helping" going to come back and haunt you over and over (Sharon's story)?

2. What other resources are available to solve the problem? In other words, are you just begging to have your guilt button pushed? How many times did you tell your kids, as a form of punishment, "Wait 'til I tell your father [mother] what you did!"?

You can use the same kind of ploy today, but without the punishment angle. Try this: "I hear what you're saying, but it sounds like something you should take up with your father [mother]!" This takes you off the guilt trip in two ways: First, it says, "I'm not going to jump right in and respond and rescue you. I want some thinking time." Second, it takes you out of the middle if you are being used as a go-between with another parent and allowing your guilt to accept responsibility for someone else's actions.

This doesn't mean you are getting rid of your own guilt just by shoving it off onto the other parent. It means you are not going to own what isn't yours. An example shows how that "owning" can keep you on a guilt trip.

Suppose your son, having had too much to drink, got into a mammoth shouting, pushing, maybe even hitting argument with his father. The scene was terrible, and you wished it had never happened. The next day, with the alcohol out of the picture, your son approaches you to help him patch things up with Dad.

"I was drinking too much, Mom," he says. "I'm afraid I said some pretty rough things to Dad last night."

Before you can even comment on that, he adds, "But that's *nothing* compared to how you and Dad were mixing it up Saturday night! My God, I thought you were going to kill him!"

As you are about to respond and defend yourself from that statement, he gives the final push to your guilt button to start you on the trip: "Talk to Dad, will you, Mom? I'm late for work!"

Neat, huh? The old you would respond to the part of what Junior said about your fight with your husband. You would use the guilt that was generated by that to own responsibility for his beef with his father.

The new you, however, refuses to fall into the trap and says, "I feel that's something you should take up with your father!" Get it? You don't even have to start on the guilt trip if you refuse to get on the train in the first place. Notice that your new-you reply doesn't even acknowledge your son's attempt to divert attention from his transgression to yours. Thus, you avoid having to defend your own actions, which often clouds the issues at hand and prevents *any* confrontation of the alcohol involvement. In other words, what transpired between you and the boy's father, as bad as it really may have been, has absolutely nothing to do with the manner in which *he* behaved while under the influence.

Finally, be cautious of doing something that will put you on a guilt trip because of something someone else may have said to you. You are *very* susceptible to suggestions such as, "If she were *my* daughter, I would give her the money! Many's the time I regretted having not helped Sally more—now that she's gone [maybe just married, not dead], I just don't feel needed!"

Boy, you can bite right into that one! The very idea that you might not be *needed* anymore can make you willing to do most anything. The guilt trip gets rolling faster than you can peel off those twenty-dollar bills to stuff into your child's hands! You see, you are playing very old tapes as parents. These tapes have to be replaced with brand-new ones. The "Promises to Make to Yourself" list and the tools discussed subsequently are new tapes that will help you take the responsibilities that are rightfully yours and throw away those that you should never own.

Don't think you are going to get off these guilt trips overnight, because you aren't. But continually practicing will help you develop the skills necessary to cope with the alcohol issue confronting your offspring and avoid clouding it with all kinds of irrelevant issues.

Dedicate yourself to taking all kinds of wonderful trips that you've always looked forward to, even if they are just fantasy. But stay away from the most realistic trip that you have been taking many times each day, week, and month of your parenthood—the guilt trip!

7
• • •
Setting
the Limits

"What do *you* think ought to be acceptable behavior in this house?"

"What rights do we have to pick and choose your friends?"

"What are the hours that you plan to keep while you're living here? We have a *right* to know!"

Do these sound like questions that you have either asked or wanted to ask your child? The ability of parents to set limits becomes a useful strategy for dealing with the present and future relationship between you and the alcohol-abusing young adult in your family. But it's hard work; it's difficult to make the distinction between what is legitimately *some* of your business and what is *none* of your business!

The truth of the matter is that a little bit of both elements come into play. Once there is evidence of an alcohol-abusing youngster living in the house, you automatically feel that you have to lower the boom. But it's also important to remember that suddenly tightening your grip can only lead to increased use of alcohol, particularly if you have been running a pretty loose ship for many years. The answer is to begin to set limits that are reasonable and that make the youngster begin to understand that you must do *something* to contribute to his or her program of getting well.

"Things just *can't* go on the way they have been, Brad. You and we both have to be willing to make some changes!"

This statement reflects a reasonable approach to a re-examination of lifestyles by parents and the abuser. It's obvious that simply going along on the same old path isn't going to work anymore. Even Brad can understand that much. But what are the limits that can safely be set as being reasonable and not just some sort of "punishment" for alcoholic behavior?

This calls for the first of many family conferences that you will need to hold throughout the process of getting well. You simply can't tell a twenty-three-year-old that he or she has to be in the house by one or even two in the morning. That kind of thing is reserved for teens and preteens. But do you have the right to say, "Brad, when you come in so late it disturbs your mother and me, and as long as you're living here we'll need to establish some hours that are acceptable to us all!"?

No mention is made of the fact that Brad might be staying out late drinking; what needs to be established is that he will not be allowed to keep such late hours because he is disturbing others. As long as Brad wants to keep taking your generous offer of room (and board, probably), he needs to abide by the house rules, rules that will apply to everyone, not just the alcohol abuser. And that's the key to setting limits. They must be created on the basis of what is acceptable behavior to you, the parents. Brad doesn't have to abide by your rules; he has the option of getting back out on his own. But as long as he *does* stay under your roof, he must understand that you are not running a freewheeling hotel. Brad may try to rebel; he may try to hook you into some sort of new guilt trip. But he also has the option of getting out on his own, and this is where you can confront him with the consequences of his alcoholic behavior. You might tell him that his drinking has caused the financial difficulties that make it necessary for him to live with you again in the first place.

"You're welcome to stay here while you're getting yourself together, Brad, but we are not going to make it any easier for you to continue the way you have been!"

You, the parent, are helping the youngster by tightening things up a bit. You are manifesting both care and concern but are also establishing that things are going to be different from before. If Brad starts to give you a lot of static about his being old enough to know when he should come in, it's time to remind him that his alcoholic behavior has caused him to lose some of the privileges that might have been his if he had come home under different circumstances.

In other words, there is a considerable difference between Brad's disturbing the household because he arrives home at some ungodly hour from a job and his doing so while pouring himself into the house after a drinking spree.

So the family has a conference to ask what will be considered acceptable as an hour for Brad to arrive home. We are assuming that he is back home because he has gotten into trouble with alcohol and has turned to you for help. You are more than willing to give your help, letting him stay with you while he seeks treatment, AA, individual counseling, or a combination of all things to put his alcohol abuse in remission. But your banner cry has to be, "We must make changes in the way things have been done!"

So, what have we learned from the example of Brad? You have set limits in these ways:

1. You have defined the fact that other people are to be taken into consideration, not just Brad.
2. While your house is open, it is open on a *temporary* basis, only while Brad is getting help.

3. You are, as a family unit, interested in seeing changes in lifestyle; the old ways are what got Brad into trouble.

4. Reasonable hours for returning home are not just *requested;* they are *expected.*

Notice that there is a little hook in one of the limits that have been set—the fact that Brad can stay with you while he is in treatment. It's too easy for parents to want to slip back into the old ways; it becomes too easy to refill the empty nest that was created when the last kid left home. Parents have a tendency to forget the word *temporary* when reopening their doors to one who has left home for a life of his own.

The problem with weakening on this issue is that you lose much of the clout for getting help for the alcoholic. You must, therefore, learn to say, "You can stay with us, and you are welcome. In return, you are expected to seek help for your alcohol problem."

Let's look at another area of limit-setting that may be the most difficult for you to bring into focus: peer group pressure. This is the limit that addresses the question we asked in the beginning: "What rights do we have to pick and choose your friends?"

Plainly stated, no one wants to give up his or her friends. Nor does the alcoholic or alcohol abuser want to give up his or her *best* friend: the bottle. But both may have to go before the person can get well. Your problem lies in meeting the resistance that will be forthcoming when you tell an adult child that he or she needs to "stay away from so-and-so" because that person is a heavy drinker and will just "get you into trouble."

What has to be reinforced is the truism that *some* changes must be made for wellness to occur. One of those changes might have to be expressed this way: "You need to find a new set of friends, ones that don't drink or at least don't drink as heavily as your current group."

Your abuser is going to fight you hard on this one! After all, *everybody* he or she knows drinks. What you are attempting to do is help him or her select friends who don't have the same problems with alcohol as your abuser. Again, your only real clout in setting this limit is the fact that the young adult is living with you, which definitely puts you in a temporary position of power. You can say that you will not allow certain people in your home, even though that may sound almost as if you are reverting to early childhood disciplines.

If you are contributing financially in other ways, say to the cost of the abuser's treatment, or you are simply augmenting his or her cash position while the abuser is seeking help, you simply have to play that trump card! You may have to threaten to cut off certain funds unless your child stops seeing friends you have identified as threats to continuing sobriety.

Where are the new friends to be found? Alcoholics Anonymous will be a primary source, particularly if care has been taken to select a group that appears to be made up largely of young people involved in the recovering process. The treatment center or program where you and your youngster are seeking help is the most natural source of new friends. Here, your son or daughter already is actively involved with other people seeking treatment, and they are facing the same problems of needing new friends.

When one couple, Paul and Sandra Vandenburg, were going through this situation with a son who was in treatment, they applied parental pressure in this way:

Sandra was always available to babysit her grandson, the product of son Charles and the wife from whom he was separated. When it was Charles's time to have his son for a visit, he would go to his wife's home, pick up the boy, and return to his parents' home, where he was living while trying to get himself through his treatment program for alcoholism.

The problem occurred when Charles just wanted to "dump" his son on Sandra for the night and then be free to go out with his buddies. For a long time Sandra and Paul didn't say anything; they were tickled to death to have their little grandson for one or even two nights, if his mother would allow a longer visit.

When it became apparent that they were simply *enabling* Charles to go right on with his life as if nothing had happened, they were faced with a dilemma. They brought the problem to their group, and after a lengthy session the Vandenburgs made a decision. They would confront Charles with what he was doing, based strictly on his unwillingness to make peer group changes.

They told their son that he was "just dumping" his child on them to go back to the bowling alley with his old gang. Charles responded in the expected fashion: "But Mom, I don't drink with the others! I just go to bowl and be with my friends! Besides, you and Dad are always saying you never get enough of Jeffy, anyhow!"

But Paul and Sandra knew that if Charles continued to associate with this hard-core group of drinkers, who had all had severe drinking problems of their own, then the possibilities of his slipping were going to increase. Many of his friends had been cited for drunken driving while coming home from the bowling alley; some had been involved in fights serious enough for bystanders to summon the police, and one or two of the group were having quite a difficult time with their marriages. But Charles had hit a strong point, an emotional one. He had pushed Paul's, and particularly Sandra's, emotional "hot buttons." They did love having their grandson Jeff visit as often as possible, and they always looked forward to the times when his mother would extend one-night visits into full weekends. But they knew they had to fight back for the sake of their son's wellness and for their own.

"We will not continue to babysit Jeffy, Charles, if you are just going to go on with your old ways!" they admonished. "It's important that you spend time with your son, and it's even *more* important that you find other things and other friends for your leisure time!"

Charles was not happy. He saw his parents' hard line as being just a way to tighten their control over him. After all, he was an adult, and he was being treated like a child. He told them so: "You're just trying to force me to go to an AA meeting or only go out with the people in my group! I don't even *know* some of them very well!"

But Paul and Sandra held their ground, relying on the power of limit-setting to help them: "No, Charles, we are not forcing you to do either of those things. What we are saying is we won't make it easy for you to keep on hanging out at the bowling alley!"

It was a tough decision and it *was* a hard line, particularly since Charles began to test his own power in the household by pushing a certain button even harder: "I'll just tell Char [his wife] to keep Jeff! I'm not going to be forced to do anything!"

"That's entirely up to you, Son," said his mother. "It will hurt us a lot not to be able to have Jeffy as often as we have, but we are going to stand by our decision."

Charles went so far as to threaten to move out of the house, but the harsh reality was that he couldn't afford a place of his own, and his wife, Charlene, was not yet ready for a reconciliation. He was playing his final ace, and his parents still had trump cards left.

Paul and Sandra reported to their group that Charles was very angry with them; he had lapsed into sullenness. His therapist took several calls from him canceling one appointment after another, and he failed to show up for his regular group. He was not drinking, however, and the Vandenburgs were prepared to ride out the storm.

At the end of the second week it was Charles's time to have his son again. Not a word was said about Paul and Sandra changing their plans to babysit, and nothing was said about Charles "going out with the gang." He picked up Jeffy from his wife's home and returned to his parents' house.

"Mom, I scheduled an appointment with Linda [his therapist] for Saturday morning. It was the only time I could get. Can you watch Jeffy for me?"

Sandra assured Charles that she was always willing to sit

with her grandson, particularly when it was helpful to Charles's treatment. She was prepared for Charles's next volley: "If it's OK, Mom, when I'm finished with Linda I'm going to see Frankie and Steve. Steve got a new car, and I said I'd help check it out. I'll be home by four."

The limit-setting was being tested. Frankie and Steve were two of the most notorious beer drinkers in Charles's bowling group, and Sandra knew it. But she also had been in treatment herself long enough to know the difference between helping and enabling and how to keep the limit firmly set.

"That's fine, Charles. I have [she should have said *we* to include Paul] no objection to your doing that. That's a whole lot different from spending all night with them at the bowling alley!"

Charles pointed out to his mother that the "guys still might have a beer or two" while they were working on the car. But Sandra reminded him that she was not a policewoman, that she wasn't going to dog his footsteps twenty-four hours a day, and that he had the responsibility for his own behavior.

It was a small victory. Charles was not yet ready to give up his boyhood chums, and he might never do that. But he had accepted the limits that were placed on him by his parents. He was going to have to *do something for his wellness* to get help from his mother. Going to see his therapist was a step back toward treatment for Charles. Sandra was also giving in a step or two: Charles was not cutting himself off entirely from the bowling group, but he was seeing them in a different environment and under more controlled circumstances. She was rewarding Charles by caring for his son, which of course was a reward for her too since she loved doing it. The difference was that Sandra was not enabling Charles to continue behavior that was detrimental to his recovery. She knew that he wouldn't go from a session with his therapist right to drinking with his friends. If his friends did have a beer or two, Charles was at least removed from the normal environment of the bowling alley. He knew that he had to be home by a certain hour as promised. Sandra put in a little safeguard just to set the limits a little further.

"Your Dad and I are going furniture shopping with Kevin and Maxie [close friends]. We'll take Jeffy with us, but we're going to come back and leave him with you so the four of us can go out to dinner together."

The limits were clearly established. Charles had not been forced either to go to a meeting or to give up his friends altogether. He had made a small change, and whether he would continue to expand on that change remained to be seen. It was a small standoff that had become a rather large victory. Sandra and Paul had gained strength in realizing that they must always be on guard against enabling Charles to avoid his own responsibilities.

Charles had realized that there was such a thing as compromise without losing too much face. He had given a little and received a little. If he were to try to push the established limits set by his parents, he would find them taking a little stronger and harder stand. The fact that he should seek new friends through AA or his therapy group would be reinforced in his session with his therapist. It would take some more time for Charles to become comfortable with this idea, but it *would* and *did* happen!

The parents had made it abundantly clear that they would not allow themselves to be "dumped on," but that they stood ready to help in any area that would advance their son's overall treatment. Let's take a tally of the points won by each side:

1. Sandra and Paul scored a point for limiting the activity they would babysit for: "yes" for a visit with friends under more controlled conditions, "no" for unlimited bowling alley outings.

2. Charles scored a point for rescheduling his therapy appointment, thus showing he was still motivated to get treatment.

3. Charles got another point for assuming some care for his own son as a priority over whatever else he wanted to do.
4. Sandra scored again for not assuming responsibility *if* Charles were to slip and drink.
5. Sandra also scored by realizing that she has a little give-and-take built into her limit-setting; the fact that she didn't let her emotional hot buttons get pushed was a decided plus.

So, both parties profit by setting limits. And it can be just the beginning of a new understanding between the parents and the young adult who is abusing alcohol. There was no need to resort to threats of cutting off any support, either financial or moral. Quite the contrary; the setting of limits allows a new, stronger relationship to be built. It is one that takes mutual respect for each other's feelings into stride. It says, "I will go this far and no further with you." And the receiver of such a message can reply with, "I understand the terms; I accept at least *part* of them and will abide by the conditions that have been set."

The idea of setting limits isn't just for young adults who have returned home to live; it also applies to the alcohol-abusing teenager who has never left home. Take the example of a young man named Chris.

Chris had been in trouble because of his beer drinking with school buddies. His homework was consistently late, and he had been disciplined at school several times, but no one had really put a finger on the fact that Chris was using alcohol to cover some very high anxiety about a pending operation.

For some time it had been apparent that a previously set shoulder bone, broken as the result of a mid-winter skiing accident, was not healing properly. Chris and his parents had been told by the attending surgeon that it looked as if the operation would have to be repeated and that Chris would need to go back into the hospital.

But Chris and his parents and two younger brothers lived in a frenetic world. Everyone was really "too busy" to schedule time out for this new operation. The surgeon had said it could wait "a few more months, three at the most," before there would be a pressing need to reset some shoulder screws. The family, with Chris at the helm, set a date in mid-March. In the meantime Chris began drinking more, and neglecting his homework and staying out too late on nights when he should have been home at a "decent hour." No one wanted to set limits on Chris's behavior.

His mother, Pat, did not like the new, harder beer-drinking crowd Chris had taken up with, but she only admonished him to "try to get home earlier." When Chris's father, Lloyd, became angered over household chores that were continually neglected, the family buck was passed for "somebody to do something" about Chris.

A birthday party for a girlfriend of Chris's friend was held at Chris's house, with everyone's permission. The beer flowed all too freely, and parents of some of the young people complained angrily to Pat about "your kid, the beer guzzler!"

When Pat and Lloyd confronted Chris about his drinking, his total lack of responsibility, and all the other "garbage" they had been saving, they imposed harsh rules. Chris was to give up "those hoodlums" who had become his friends. There were to be curfew hours during the week and only slightly extended weekend hours.

Chris was to have his homework signed, something that hadn't been asked of him since seventh grade when he had had a rather lackadaisical attitude. But *nothing* was done to attack what was making Chris keep drinking more and more beer! It was as if the pending operation was on the back burner of everyone's mind, and Chris's parents were out to control his behavior by tightening screws of a different kind. When Chris grudgingly accepted the new and more rigid behavior code he just kept drinking—alone, in his room, or quite hard and fast during the limited hours in which he was allowed out of the house.

When his behavior continued to deteriorate, Pat consulted the school counselor, who recommended a therapist. The therapist in turn picked up on the drinking behavior, and Chris and his parents ended up in a treatment center for an assessment of the problem.

When therapy divulged Chris's very real fear about the surgery, the fact that he was deathly afraid that his shoulder would never be right again (at least right enough for the skiing he so loved), the reason for his accelerated beer drinking began to surface. Coupled with some known alcoholism among grandparents, it became apparent that Chris was getting into real trouble with his drinking.

The family did some hard work to set realistic limits for the young man. His friends were no longer blamed for his problems, and the selection of them was up to him. Pat and Lloyd learned to begin treating Chris as he deserved to be treated. If Chris acted in a responsible fashion, his parents assumed he was interested in getting well, and they therefore treated him in a responsible fashion. Irresponsible behavior on Chris's part, no matter in what area it occurred, was treated as an *unwell* sign, and Chris was treated as such.

Parents and son readjusted their limit-setting to base it on Chris's willingness to treat himself as someone who was facing a drinking problem, and on the understanding that Chris was using and abusing his alcohol as a sedative to numb the fear of the surgery he was facing. Family treatment became an important tool for everyone to get to know one another better and to set realistic rules for behavior, based on giving much of the responsibility for those rules to Chris himself. He could choose his own friends; if they helped him get into trouble, then he—not his parents—had to adjust the circle of friends. If homework didn't get done, there was no more writing of phony notes, as Pat had done in the past to bail Chris out. He took his own consequences.

As Pat and Lloyd learned to set limits with Chris, they learned to set limits for themselves. They realized that they had let family communication slip to an all-time low, not only with Chris but with his two brothers as well. Together they determined how to cut their own activities down to allow more family time, and, as a result, everyone prospered.

Chris had his operation, and everything went well. His beer drinking ceased, and the family continued in treatment to deal with many issues that were jumping out at them once alcohol was out of the picture. The limit-setting continued for all concerned, but as a tool for better communications between them rather than as a means of punishment.

Probably one of the strongest points for learning to set limits is the experience of the past. Whatever was happening before just wasn't working! It soon becomes obvious that, in trying not to hurt anyone's feelings and to get themselves off that guilt trip, parents are willing to put up with almost anything. It's almost as if the parents have been crying out to receive even *more* punishment at the hands of their alcoholic young adult than before! It is as if the more punishment the parent can handle, the easier the guilt trip will be—something that *never* happens. The guilt trip just gets worse, and so does the alcoholic!

Each time it becomes necessary to establish new ground rules, to set new limits, there is a golden opportunity for family conferences. These can be real icebreakers among family members who have found their relationship strained to the breaking point; they can be springboards to a family unity that has been missing for some time.

One thing has to be kept clearly in sight. When setting limits, the *self-respect* of all parties has to be a prime consideration. It's too easy just to try to make the alcoholic "eat crow" or wear the proverbial "sackcloth and ashes." The setting of limits establishes the theme that you, the parents, recognize the disease that is causing these problems and are simply saying, "We have to try something different, because what we have done in the past simply didn't work."

Use the setting of limits as frequently as you see the need to point out what your young person's alcoholic behavior has meant to him or her. Use the tool of setting limits as a way for the recovering person to save face in some small way while at the same time adjusting to a more stringent code of behavior.

The rewards for everyone concerned are great. In the long run you will find it easier to deal with the alcoholic young person when limits have been set. As you will see in the next chapter, you and your alcoholic child are going to learn to enter into a contract of behavior that will be the guideline you both will follow for the term of the alcoholic's recovery program.

It's never too late to set limits! That's why we have thermostats on heaters and controls on vehicles—to proceed as safely as possible along life's paths, in as comfortable a fashion as is possible for *all* parties concerned!

8
• • •
Drawing Up
a Contract

"I'm not signing any damn contract!"

"What do you think we're running here? A union shop?"

"I'm your *daughter*, for God's sake! You make me feel like a steel worker!"

So once again you, the parent, feel like you're trying to start a new Nazi regime or worse! And yet the idea of having a contract between you and your alcoholic young adult makes a lot of sense. Things have, after all, changed. There you were, thinking that all of your own brood were finally out on their own, when this personal tragedy of alcoholism or alcohol abuse struck.

Suppose a young adult wants to move back into the family home while he or she tackles the alcohol problem? Are you going to say "no"? In the last chapter, Charles was a good example; he didn't have much of a choice after his wife ordered him to leave their house. He was unemployed and didn't have the funds for an apartment, so his parents took him back in. What if the same thing happened to you?

Suppose, however, that your young adult was single and living in his or her own apartment, perhaps in another city. The alcohol problem rears its ugly head, and you are caught between two tough choices: "Do I let her move back in and disrupt our life?" or "Do I let her stay where she is and start paying her rent until she gets on her feet?"

Why does she need her rent paid? Because her alcohol abuse has probably led her into serious financial difficulty. This is so common that I include it as a matter of fact and not just as some made-up example. Most of the young adults I have worked with as a therapist come into treatment in severe financial difficulty and have had to rely on the help of their parents to weather financial storms.

The problem with allowing your young person to stay where she is while you just pick up the rent tab, or at least part of it, is that you probably won't have any control over her getting any *help* for her alcohol problem. That's the key issue, and it becomes a more powerful weapon than you've had before. The young person doesn't want to have to ask you for anything but is caught on the horns of a dilemma. She needs help, has little or no money, and is forced into asking you for both. Your weapon is to refuse to give money or provide a place to live *unless* a serious effort is made to get help for the alcohol problem.

It may sound harsh for me to refer to "weapons" and your "power" to back your own kids into a corner, but that's what we're talking about here—war! You will be joining in a fight to help your child save his own life, and it will take all of the weapons in your arsenal, plus the new ones introduced in this book.

No contract should be loaded against one side or the other; that's not fair, and that's not what's intended. But try to think of this in terms of labor and management for just a moment. When two sides sit down across the table from each other, supposedly the idea is to come up with an agreement, something that will get the production line moving again.

I tell people in therapy with whom I'm working that they need to ask themselves the same question: "What will it take to make this thing work? What do I have to *take* on one issue and what do I want to *give* on another?"

I know of no better way for parents and child to negotiate than to adopt the same kinds of parameters that come into play between union and management. You both have rights; you both believe that you may have the best points of view. But if either side decides that it is more important to be right than it is to get a contract, nothing will change.

So, to begin with, don't stack the deck in favor of you and your spouse just because you are parents. Start with the premise that it's not really important who is right or wrong; what's important is to arrive at a new way of doing things.

If the young person is in treatment and living in the parents' home, some things have to be different; both sides need to accept that for the contract to work. As we discussed in the last chapter, you may be dealing with someone who has not had to ask permission to stay out at night or who certainly *never* checked with you about friends.

But your child's old way of doing things obviously didn't work, or he or she wouldn't be in treatment and back at home with you. Again, contracts work best when the young adult has moved back into the parents' home. This method has been used successfully when the young adult lives in the same city but still maintains his or her own apartment or house, but it's very hard to know whether the contract is being violated in these cases.

For our purposes, then, let's assume the situation as follows: Your daughter has never left home. She has an alcohol/drug problem and is going to get treatment. Take Marabeth as an example.

Marabeth is twenty-one years old. She graduated from high school as an average student—not particularly studious but not down in the academic cellar. Marabeth is extremely pretty, and that's probably one of her downfalls. Her doting parents have given in to her every whim and have seen to it that she has wanted for nothing, within their means. They have also pampered their other two children.

Marabeth's good looks have led her to believe, through her high school years at least, that that's all it will take for her in life: good looks and very little else. She tried experimenting with several different kinds of the "usual" drugs, such as marijuana and cocaine. She used alcohol only on a "partying" basis in high school, and the cocaine was not a regular indulgence for her, but she liked the high she got whenever she used either or both. Marabeth dated a lot, and her striking good looks made her a favorite with the best and fastest-moving crowd of guys in her school.

Marabeth's parents, Ted and Elaine, were concerned about Marabeth's apparent lack of interest in college. She wasn't like the other girls, who seemed to be looking forward to getting out of high school and going on to college, particularly away from the city where they lived. Marabeth kept her grade average high enough to make her eligible, but she just didn't seem to be "motivated," as Ted remarked.

Marabeth had always worked, first at the usual baby-sitting jobs that came to her from the time she was thirteen. Then she worked part-time at the "mom and pop" grocery store that was in her neighborhood. It gave her a sense of freedom to have her own spending money. She certainly didn't have to work, as Ted and Elaine were both affluent enough to provide more than amply for their family's needs and many luxuries as well.

Marabeth wanted a sports car, and that was her real motivation. She was saving all of her money for a late-model sports car that had struck her fancy. She bugged Ted about it constantly, and he had agreed to match her funds with the necessary amount to buy the car, picking up the difference as a graduation present.

When Marabeth graduated with her class, she didn't even apply to one of the state colleges. She wanted to work, and for her work was a reward system all its own. She had gotten the sports car as promised, but soon it was no longer new. She had the car just three months before she wrecked it coming home from work late one night.

Ted and Elaine were just grateful that Marabeth had no injuries other than a broken ankle—she could have been killed. When Ted and Elaine confronted Marabeth about whether she had been partying after work at the restaurant where she was employed she admitted that she had had "one or two" drinks with some of her friends. Her parents admonished her about the dangers of drinking and driving, something they had done with all of their kids. To Marabeth it was just another lecture; she had heard it all before, even in high school. It was no big deal for her; she had survived the wreck, and now the most important thing was to replace her car.

The idea of another new car became an obsession to Marabeth. It was all she talked about and all she *ever* talked to her parents about. She began to double up on her jobs, working at a family restaurant on the morning/lunch shift, taking three or four hours off to "catch some rays," then changing and heading back to a very popular restaurant-bar where she worked as a cocktail waitress, making very good tips.

Ted couldn't say "no" to his daughter. He was a massive enabler in that respect, and he jumped the gun on Marabeth's attempts to save enough to replace her wrecked car.

Ted didn't want to appear to be too much of a doting father, so he got around the problem by doing this: He didn't *exactly* buy Marabeth a new car before she had the funds; he bought his wife a new car and then gave her late-model vehicle to Marabeth. It wasn't good enough! Marabeth pleaded, hounded, and generally made life a living hell for the whole family until Ted and Elaine allowed her to trade in her mother's car for the exact model she had had before.

The outcome of Marabeth's ranting and raving and generally spoiled behavior was obvious. Ted gave in and signed the title over to Marabeth. She could do what she wanted, but he wouldn't make up any cash difference. She didn't need his help; she had the money squirreled away and was able to get a newer model of the same kind of car she had had before. She was in a state of ecstasy, and Ted and Elaine were also delighted, telling themselves and their friends that Marabeth had "earned" the car herself, even though that was really stretching the enabling Ted had accomplished in the first place.

Marabeth's alcohol problems were increasing through all of this. She was drinking more and more and running with the kind of crowd that thought nothing of using both cocaine and alcohol, not just as party enhancers but as the reason for partying. She had to call in sick more and more often to one job or the other, and over a period of months it became painfully clear to Ted and Elaine that their daughter had an alcohol problem. Marabeth was also aware of it, and to her credit it was she, not her parents, who sought treatment help.

So the whole family entered treatment—Marabeth in her regular program of recovery and Ted and Elaine involving themselves in all aspects of treatment, including their parents' group therapy. Things went along pretty smoothly for Marabeth and the parents for several weeks; things were good among all the family members. Then the relapse happened.

Marabeth "broke training," mixing some drugs with alcohol, and had another car accident. Miraculously, no one was hurt in this wreck either, but Marabeth's car was once again nearly totaled. Also once again, she started her plaintive cry of the importance of having another sports car to replace the one she had lost. Ted wasn't going to do it, but Marabeth's attitude was so different that he listened to her request: "It's different, Daddy, from before! I'm in treatment, and even though I had a slip, I'm getting help for my problem! Besides, with the kinds of hours I work, I need my own car."

Ted and Elaine looked at the estimates for repairing her car and thought that the expense wouldn't be justified. But Elaine was changing her tune about their running out and getting Marabeth another new car.

"You can use my car, Marabeth, until we see how you get along with your treatment program and how serious you are about your alcoholism!"

That's how the contract between Marabeth and her parents came into being. Other members of the parents' group had used a contract before, quite successfully, and Ted and Elaine liked the idea of putting something in writing.

Marabeth didn't dig the idea at all! It was demeaning to her, and she complained bitterly, both to her therapist and to other members of her recovery group. To her peer group of friends she didn't even mention the idea. It was bad enough that they knew she was in treatment and had somewhat excluded her from many social activities so as to not tempt her with the alcohol and drugs that flowed freely at such occasions.

But Ted, and particularly Elaine, held firm. There *would* be a contract, and furthermore, Ted and Elaine were going to see that the contract was witnessed by Marabeth's therapist. This last piece of action is something that we at Gateway Treatment Center have found very useful. It gives an official stamp to the contract and closes up some loopholes for all parties concerned.

The plum that Ted held out for drawing up the contract in the first place *was* a new car. If Marabeth stuck to the terms of the contract, Ted would get her another new car. That was motivation enough for Marabeth, and she agreed that the three of them would sit down and draw up such an agreement.

All three were asked (by the therapist who was guiding this activity) to set down their terms, individually and without help from the others. In other words, Ted, Elaine, and Marabeth all came in with a list of their demands or terms for the drawing up of the contract. As you can imagine, the battle lines were pretty clearly drawn, reverting to traditional parent-child issues.

Some of the things Ted wanted:

1. Marabeth was to come home between her two jobs.
2. She was to report all of her earnings on a weekly basis. He wanted her to account for her money.
3. She was not to borrow anyone else's car. If her mother needed her car, then Marabeth had to get a ride with friends.
4. He wanted her in at specified times at night.
5. He wanted her to quit the bar job.

Elaine had a slightly different set of demands. More of her concerns were for Marabeth's treatment:

1. Elaine wanted Marabeth to start on monitored Antabuse, something she had refused in the past.
2. She wanted Marabeth to tell her (Elaine) when her individual therapy appointments were, so she could make sure Marabeth kept them.
3. She wanted her to quit *both* jobs.
4. She wanted Marabeth to enter conjoint therapy sessions with her. This was because Elaine felt some hostility from Marabeth.
5. Elaine didn't want Marabeth to use *her* car for anything except going to work and her therapy sessions.
6. Elaine wanted to know whom Marabeth was with and whom she was going to see.

In other words, Elaine was going to tighten the screws!

Marabeth turned out to have the most reasonable terms for her part of the contract agreement:

1. Marabeth wanted to take the Antabuse.
2. She didn't want anyone to monitor her taking it!
3. She wanted to use her mother's car for all her needs, but only if it was convenient for her mother. That is, she would be happy to drop her mom at wherever her appointment was, then go on and use the car herself.
4. Marabeth wanted some curfews. She *wanted* to be

told when she had to be home! Her reasoning was sound; she wanted an excuse to have to leave and get home, particularly if there were signs of a heavy party in the making.

5. She wanted to do some work around home to earn money and to allow her to give up the restaurant job.
6. She wanted to get her new car now and make payments directly to her father. She would give him her savings for the downpayment.
7. She wanted to disclose her alcoholism to her employer. Marabeth thought it would be helpful if "they" knew.

So, all in all, everyone brought pretty good points to the family bargaining table. Nothing seemed to be so cast in cement that it couldn't be changed or altered until it was acceptable.

There wasn't anything fancy about the contract. Ted dragged out one of his many yellow legal pads, and they drafted the document. Here's what finally emerged:

CONTRACT AMONG MARABETH, TED, AND ELAINE

1. Marabeth will take Antabuse, and Elaine will monitor her taking it. She will take it in the mornings.
2. Marabeth will have weeknight hours: She will be home one hour after getting off work. Weekend arrangements are made on a week-by-week basis, but Elaine must know whom she is with.
3. Marabeth can use Elaine's car for work and for one social function per week.
4. Marabeth would tell her employer about her alcoholism and sign a release form allowing the treatment center to disclose progress reports to the employer (who was very supportive of Marabeth's treatment).
5. Marabeth would trade her bar job for a combination food service/bar service job at the employer's other

restaurant. This way she could give up the straight bar service job. She now had *one* job but at less total money.

6. Ted would double his contribution toward a new car because of this new job arrangement. *However:*
7. Marabeth would not get her new car for at least three months.
8. She was to remain drug- and alcohol-free; no relapses during this time period, or the car purchase would be pushed back another month for each episode.
9. Marabeth was to keep all appointments, including her small group therapy sessions. (She had been "ditching" them.)
10. She was not to borrow anyone else's car under *any* circumstances. If she slipped and either drank or took pills or other substances and could not drive, she was to call home. Someone would come after her no matter what time of night it was.

The matter of the conjoint therapy sessions between Marabeth and her mother would naturally take care of itself in the regular structure of her treatment program, and there was no need to make a separate contract item out of that.

Ted, Elaine, and Marabeth all signed the agreement and took it in for Marabeth's therapist to see. Ted and Elaine made a copy and, with Marabeth's consent, shared the terms with their parents' group.

This is a good example of how some basic hostility from the young adult and some very well-hidden hostility from the parents could be seen and dealt with as genuine anger.

The anger was acknowledged by all three, but they agreed to handle those issues in the regular course of therapy. In the meantime, here was a working document that could help ease anxieties while Marabeth's main priority remained the treatment of her disease.

Remember, a contract is not drawn up as a form of punishment. It's designed only to be a tool, a method that says, "We need something different in our game plan!" The fact that you can draw up a contract at all is based on your mastery of the tools you have learned about in previous chapters: the difference between helping and enabling and the realization that new methods have to be explored as a means of treating the disease of alcoholism.

The relationship between you and the alcoholic young adult is a totally different one when he or she moves back into your home, particularly under the circumstances that we have been describing. Marabeth had never left home, so the contract was used as a method of determining one of the parameters under which she would be *allowed* to continue living at home and staying in treatment.

The added wedge of informing her employer was good. It helped strengthen Marabeth's program of recovery, and it gave Elaine, particularly, another source of support for helping Marabeth stay on the sober/drug-free path.

Ted had the hardest time. He could find no traceable alcoholism in his family tree, and he himself rarely drank. He had a hard time understanding how the disease had struck his daughter in the first place. The contract made it unnecessary for him to deal with anything more than the immediate problem—keeping Marabeth alcohol- and drug-free and out of car accidents! Later in therapy the vital family link *was* discovered, and Ted felt much better about accepting his daughter's disease as an inherited genetic problem instead of something he had caused.

Working out the contract also can bring young adults and parents closer together even if the subject is a difficult one to start with. It certainly doesn't replace something like the family's going skiing together or even watching a football game or working together on a jigsaw puzzle. But it does force you to sit down as three individuals and hammer out a single document that represents all three points of view.

The biggest thing to remember is it is a proven tool. The contract you draw up, sign, and deliver may be the most important document for family wellness that you will ever have. Take time to work on it. Make it work for you!

9
● ● ●
Setting the Consequences

Now you have some kind of contract with your alcoholic youngster, and things appear to be all "peaches and cream." Then it happens! Disaster strikes, and your contract and your heart are broken at the same time; there is a relapse.

It may be only a short drinking episode of one or two bottles of beer or it might be a night of really heavy drinking. It doesn't really matter, because drinking for the alcoholic is drinking, no matter the quantity consumed. He or she does it because it is a disease and because it can't be helped if he or she triggers that ever-present loaded mouse-trap that is THIQ.

So there you sit, heartbroken and really angry. Things were going so well, and then *this* had to happen! You probably are sitting right there across the kitchen table, asking your abusing youngster the perennial question, "*Why* did you do it?!"

Well, save yourself a lot of trouble. Stop asking why and get on with the business of asking what the young person wants to do about the relapse—and when, where, and how. I like to refer clients who constantly ask why to the Book of Job in the Old Testament.

For a whole bunch of pages Job asks why of his Creator until, finally, even heavenly patience runs out and we read a powerful admonition about questioning things we don't have any control over. The important element for you as a parent to realize is that you *do* have a contract. It was negotiated, signed, and witnessed, in good faith, and you need to make sure its terms are going to be honored.

If there had been a violation on *your* part, you can be assured that you would have heard about it! The same is true with the main clause of your contract: the one about drinking.

This particular clause is an *unwritten* one, if it was not a part of the original document that you signed. This whole contract business, after all, is predicated on the understanding that there will be no drinking or other substance abuse for the term of the contract, and hopefully for a lifetime!

But relapses *do* happen; they are a part of the disease, and in many cases a relapse can prove to be therapeutically beneficial. For a young person to look at giving up alcohol for the rest of his life is overwhelming. That's why one of the main principles of recovery, and certainly one of the main understandings of the AA program, is to admonish oneself to live life just one day at a time.

The younger the alcoholic, the more tempted he or she will be to test the system. Maybe, just maybe, the youngster thinks, he or she is the one alcoholic who can take just one drink and quit. So, the alcoholic tests the theory. If the youngster gets away with taking that one drink, he is going to try another, and soon he is drunk, just as if he had never stopped drinking in the first place. That's part of the progressive nature of the disease, and no matter how many times it's tested, it's *always* going to work the same way.

So, you are faced with figuring out what you are going to

do about this. The main clause of your contract, whether actually written or mutually understood, has been broken, and it requires some action on your part. You must not let the challenge go unanswered. If you do, before long all you will have is a worthless piece of paper that doesn't mean a thing, and you really will be back to square one!

Let's take a hypothetical scenario and see what can be done with it.

Suppose your young-adult offspring stopped at his or her favorite watering hole, quaffed a few beers, got back into the car, and started home. On the way he lost control of his car and had an accident, but it didn't involve anyone but himself.

The car ran a barricade, hit a deep hole, and tore apart the undercarriage, causing a lot of damage. The car had to be towed and repaired, and your son's insurance company would either increase his premiums or cancel his policy because of the damage and the frequency with which he has made claims.

Now what can you do? Can you take away his car? Probably not, particularly if he bought and paid for it or is making the payments himself. In fact, he may have had the car for quite some time before he came to you with his alcohol problem. Reverting to teenage discipline and demanding his keys won't work. Something else is in order, something that treats the situation more in line with the nature of your contract. If his car is disabled, he is going to need transportation. Should you provide it? If his car has been so badly damaged that it needs repairs, should you repair it? Suppose his insurance *has* been canceled. Should you shop around and find another company for him? These questions can't necessarily be answered with absolute yeses or nos. Consider the following contractual solutions.

If he needs transportation to go to his job, you could provide it by taking him to work and picking him up while his car is being repaired, which involves a lot of chauffeuring and is neither very practical nor a very serious consequence for breaking his contract. But you *could* drive him to the nearest bus stop if it's quite far away and let him fend for himself!

I have worked with parents who didn't even go that far. They knew their son was going to have to get from his home to his job in the downtown area of the city, then from there on to his college classes, which were held in an adjoining town.

They offered to loan him bus money; he refused and chose instead to hitchhike back and forth from home to job to campus. It was the parents' efforts to enforce the terms of their contract with him that paid off. They *did* drive him to all of his therapy sessions and group meetings—an ideal way to carry out the consequences of a broken contract!

You can make the same sort of compromise: "No," you will not provide him with your car for getting back and forth to non-treatment-related items, but "yes," you will assist him in making his treatment or private care appointments.

You'll get a lot of flak! Expect it and batten down the hatches. You must stand your ground, for the only real teeth in your contract are the consequences that you set when its terms are broken.

What about repairing the car? You definitely need to have it fixed, but are you the ones to phone around to get estimates? Are you the ones to foot the bill? Here, I believe the answer should be a resounding *"no."* These are direct results of alcoholic behavior and should *not* be catered to, no matter how strong the appeal!

You would probably have to lend the money for repairs, but this should be done by drawing up a promissory note. Do it for real! You can buy those printed promissory notes at most stationery stores and even drugstores. Fill in the amount of the loan, the interest rate you are going to charge, and the amount to be paid back in set monthly or weekly installments.

Remember, the more it hits his billfold, the more he will realize the consequences of breaking his contract by drinking. You may have to go a little further on the insurance angle. He may not be able to get his insurance renewed without considerable help from you. You will have to play this as close to the vest as possible, but keep drumming in the fact that all of this difficulty is a direct result of alcoholic behavior! Your ability to provide financial support cannot be taken into consideration, and you must *not* just hand out sums of money to pay the repair, insurance, or other accident-related expenses. That would be enabling at its worst!

Keep referring back to your contract; give it teeth by reinforcing the ideas that were agreed on in the first place. The object of setting consequences is not to make life totally miserable for your alcoholic, but to underline the importance you place on having a contract in the first place.

If a union member or a law partner—or, for that matter, anyone with whom you have a contract—were to break certain provisions of that contract, there would be some set of consequences. Your contract with your alcoholic is not different. It has a set of rules that all parties agree to follow; if those rules are broken, then the "piper must be paid."

You will find that the most difficult consequences for you to carry through are those related to finances and cars. Today's young adults consider financial independence and their own set of wheels paramount. When Mom or Dad threatens either of those assets, it's tough!

Often you can make the payments on your loan equal the amount of money that your son or daughter was spending on alcohol. This does not mean just the amount spent on the recent relapse, but the average amount that was being used on a weekly or monthly basis when the abuser was actively drinking.

Don't keep adding to the amount of money borrowed to repair the car. It's too easy for your son or daughter to play on your sympathies and get you to shell out more money. This defeats the purpose of having set consequences in the first place.

Continuing with our hypothetical case, suppose that you

have agreed to repair your son's car. You have told him you will not just pay for the car repair and the towing charges outright, but you *will* make a loan and present a promissory note for his signature. The amount to be paid back is directly tied to the amount of money he brings home from his job. You have done everything right so far. Now, however, he approaches you with a little idea for "consolidating" his debts. Now you are in trouble and have to be careful not to put on your "daddy or mommy wings" and rescue him once again.

"As long as you're going to loan me money to fix my car, Dad, could you let me have three hundred more so I can clean up a few other little loans? That way, I'll be sure to have plenty of cash available to make the payments to you!"

Sound reasonable? It's a real trap. You want to avoid adding "apples and oranges" here. Whatever "little" debts he may have are not *directly* related to this last accident, which was *alcohol-related*, and therefore could muddy up your contract.

He needs to feel the pinch that his use of alcohol caused, and the fact that he may also be financially in a bind from something else should be left for him to work out any way he can. You want to set consequences that are a direct result of *violation* of his contract against drinking. Everything else just clouds the issue and does very little to help him or you get a handle on realizing the consequences of alcoholic behavior.

So far, we have assumed that your alcoholic is gainfully employed. But what if the alcohol abuser doesn't have a job? Can you get him or her to sign a promissory note when there is no known source of income? Yes! Let's say the same hypothetical accident happened to your daughter. To add to all her other woes, she lost her job for one reason or another, and she is totally dependent on your generosity for survival. What to do?

Your daughter needs to work out the loan. Perhaps she can assume more and more of the household duties that you have been doing. Perhaps you are a working wife and would like to have help with the housecleaning and meal preparation.

Your daughter can assume these chores and get paid for her efforts. I recall the story of a man whose daughter was in just such a predicament. She needed a source of income to pay back the loan he was making her to repair her car, which was damaged in an alcohol-related accident. He didn't need his house cleaned or his meals prepared; he had a wife who not only was willing to do those things but considered it her contribution to their relationship, since he made quite a handsome income and she did not have to work.

The daughter *could* do something to earn money and meet some of her father's needs. He put her to work at his office in a job that really didn't require the full-time services of any other employees. He needed old files in the basement sorted, boxed, and stacked in neat rows and piles to make room for more documents.

It was a dirty, wear-your-old-clothes kind of job, and the daughter balked at the suggestion that she do it.

"No wonder you can't hire anyone to do this!" she complained. "You're just forcing me to do it because you *hate* me and because I wrecked my car."

The father, I recall, almost allowed his emotional love/ hate button to be pushed. But he stopped to think long enough to inform his daughter that she had broken her contract about drinking; *that* was the issue, and she needed to pay for her car repairs. He reemphasized that he was perfectly willing to help her get the car fixed, that he had authorized the repairs, and that he had indeed paid the bill. She owed him money for this, was going to sign a promissory note, and needed a way to pay that note.

The father pointed out that she could avoid doing the job he had offered her by going out and getting employment on her own, something she had been unsuccessful in doing in the past recent weeks. He noted further that she could also avoid doing this messy job by giving him title to her car, allowing him to sell it if he wished to recoup his considerable investment. Well! The roof really came off the house with that one!

There was no way daughter was going to give up her car! She had worked hard to get it, and until alcohol had begun wreaking havoc in her life, she had responsibly cared for her "baby," as she called it. The upshot was that the young woman had no choice. Both parents were determined that their contract would be honored; the consequences for breach had been set and were kept accordingly.

Daughter felt quite shaky from her alcohol relapse; withdrawal left her feeling little or no confidence in getting employment on her own. She took her father's job offer and began punching a time clock, doing the dirty and physically demanding work no one else wanted. She felt a lot of genuine hatred, particularly toward her father, over this issue. She told her therapist that she was also angry at her mother for not backing her instead of "taking Daddy's side." She began to berate her mother for being just a "slave" in her "master's house," and derogatory remarks of all kinds poured forth from the very angry young lady.

Then she got her first paycheck. She had assumed that her father would simply give her a lump sum when the job was completed. He didn't. He instructed his payroll department to add her as a contract employee (making her responsible for her own taxes). She was paid a fair and equitable wage, and under "deductions," she found that the amount of her loan payment to her parents had been removed. At first she was angry that her father didn't trust her to pay him what she owed him.

The father calmly asked her what sort of track record she was offering him as proof that she would honor her promissory note. Both parents then reinforced their contract by telling their daughter that, if she continued keeping her therapy appointments and fulfilling her other treatment obligations, they would allow her to assume the responsibility of making her loan payment without the automatic deduction.

93

The slick thing about how the parents handled this was what the father was doing with the pay-back money. He was putting the amount of the loan payment into a money market account that he opened in trust for his daughter. When she finally completed the work for her father he found other equally humbling tasks in his business for her to do.

She began to refer to herself among the other employees as "Cinderella," and before long she had earned not only money but deep and genuine respect from her father's other workers. She actually began to enjoy her work, finding new challenges in the many loathsome kinds of basement clean-up and humdrum tasks that were assigned her. She got a raise, went off contract employee status, and began receiving company benefits as well as having taxes deducted from her paychecks.

When a supervisor approached her father about the need for another employee to fill a receptionist position, the supervisor requested "Cindy."

"She's a willing worker and has a lot of spunk!" she told the girl's father. "She's earned a chance to move out of the basement, and I'd like to have her in the outer office!"

"Cindy" was offered the job, took it, and went on to earn several more advancements in her father's company. She never again complained about the loan payment deduction, and when Christmas of that year arrived her parents presented her with a statement of her money market account. It showed a considerable amount, with interest, and her father explained what he had been doing as she retired her loan debt.

Two things were accomplished: "Cindy" earned her self-respect and the respect of others in her father's office. She also paid off her car debt to her parents, thus facing the consequences that followed her breach of contract in the first place.

"Cindy" received an added reward in the money market fund that her parents established for her, allowing her to realize that her father did not hate her at all; he was attempting to help her without enabling her to continue alcoholic behavior. She had the opportunity to gain a good, responsible position in her father's firm without having it handed to her (as most other things in her life had been).

"Cindy" has remained chemically free; she neither uses drugs nor takes alcohol. She has continued in her aftercare program with a women's AA group and still sees her therapist on a regular, bimonthly basis, working on yet unresolved problems in her life.

Her parents remained in their parents' group, learning and passing on their experiences to newer members of their group. They learned the importance of setting consequences and sticking to them!

Everybody came out a winner in this example. And you can do the same thing over and over if you are willing to take the risks that are involved. The idea of setting consequences is probably new to you; it is to most parents who are just learning how to deal with alcoholic young people.

For so long the only way that you have dealt with inappropriate behavior has been either to punish by removing something or to allow a geographical escape (you allowed your young person to move out of the house, out of town, out of school, or whatever) to solve the problem. A what? A *geographical escape!*

If there was an alcohol/drug problem, you both assumed that things would be better elsewhere or that the problem wouldn't exist in some other city, at some other school, or in some other job.

Well, that doesn't work! The alcohol problem goes right along with the person no matter where he or she goes. What you are learning to do now is to *take a stand;* you and your young person together are learning not to run away.

The ability to draw up a contract and set consequences for the breaking of the terms of that contract is an important tool for recovery. You may want to break the rules yourself; you may want to forget about the contract "just this once"; or you may decide, "Let's give her another chance." You must learn to get tough with yourself, emotionally.

It's never easy to say "no" to a person, particularly your own child, but the ability that you develop to take a firm stand will reap great rewards for you and the alcoholic. The young person learns to realize that he or she is in total command of whether there will be good consequences or bad consequences.

It's strictly up to the abuser whether or not to break the covenants of the agreement you have hammered out together. If you keep your end of the contract, and you are willing to impose the penalties (bad consequences), then you are helping your young adult and yourself.

Failing to stick to the consequences you have set will be worse than never setting them in the first place! Set and keep consequences. Reward the keeping of that contract, and you will find rewards for yourselves!

10
• • •
Coping with Failure

"He's down in his room, drunk! My God! Is there no end to this?"

"I thought we had it whipped this time! We were so wrong!"

And so the moaning about so-called "failures" erupts throughout the living rooms and kitchens of the parents of America's alcohol-abusing young people! The "failures" are relapses and for the parents, the world seems to have grown very, very cold. All those weeks, the perfect attendance at meetings, all the work in individual and group therapy, all the AA contacts seem to "fade to black" in the depths of another night's drinking.

The discouragement is very real, and I don't discount the despair that the parents feel. It seems like so much effort has been expended by everyone in the family—and for what? The kid just goes and gets drunk again!

Well, here are some new thoughts for you to translate

into workable tools for dealing with these failures. For one thing, you must realize that in the treatment of the alcoholic a relapse is many times very beneficial.

How can this be? Suppose all of you have been strongly rejecting the idea that there is an alcohol problem. Denial in itself is one of the major stumbling blocks to successful treatment.

Perhaps your son has deluded himself into thinking that he has learned to control his drinking, particularly after several weeks or months of treatment. Perhaps you and your alcohol-abusing daughter have been regularly attending AA and Al-Anon meetings. Things have been going along just swimmingly, and then there's a relapse.

The alcoholic has been thinking about drinking for some time! It rarely just happens. We present a lecture at our treatment center called "Having a BUD (Building Up to Drink)." Its premise is that many guideposts or warning signs come into view before the person actually takes a drink. The alcoholic simply chooses to ignore those signs; he or she *chooses*, finally, to drink.

RELAPSE WARNING SIGNS

Following are the guideposts I use as a warning for "Having a BUD":

Drinking Dreams

If the recovering person is having a series of nightmares in which he or she has returned to drinking, and if these dreams continue with frequency, I believe the person's subconscious is spending far too much time thinking about drinking! As a recovering person myself, I occasionally experience these dreams even now, after years of sobriety. I still have a nightmare in which I return to smoking, even though I gave that habit a complete shove-off more than twenty years ago!

98

If your recovering person keeps having these relapse dreams, be supportive; give him or her lots of love and reinforcement for *not* having gone back to drinking.

Pushing Alcohol

Does your alcoholic always try to push the use of alcohol on you or other family members or guests in your house? Most often this pushing will be accompanied by some statement along these lines: "You don't have any problem, so why not have another?" Forcing alcohol on other people is a good warning sign that there may be a BUD in the making.

Resentment

This guidepost actually couples with the one above. During the pushing process, note the resentment in the voice and the mannerisms of the recovering person; it's almost hostile! "*You* can drink! *I* can't!" is the scream that can be detected.

Another way the abuser shows resentment is in refusing to go out (such as to a church function) because "those things are no fun" anymore! What is *really* meant is "I don't want to go because there's no fun in *anything* where you can't drink, and *I* can't drink anyhow!"

Perfectionism

If you thought there were perfect people before, you've seen nothing until you see the demands the recovering person places on himself or herself! The room is never clean enough, nor the food cooked properly. The grades in school are not good enough (even if they are very high), nor is the compliment rendered quite sincere enough!

What the recovering person is doing here is looking for a way to avoid meeting his or her extremely lofty standards, thus setting the stage for returning to drink. Simple, isn't it? Set impossible goals, then, when the goals are not reached, you *have* to drink out of disappointment!

"Pity Pot"

I elaborated on this more fully in my book, *The Joy of Being Sober* (Contemporary Books, Inc., 1984), but let's touch on it briefly here. This is the magical pot that grows wider and deeper the longer one sits on its rim! When you hear and observe your recovering person climbing back onto the "pity pot" ("Gee, I can never drink again; life's no fun!"), look out! A BUD is probably in the offing!

Overconfidence

The recovering person believes there is almost nothing that cannot be done now that he or she is sober. In itself, that's very good and helps strengthen the recovery process. But when you observe displays of this "superman" complex time and time again, it's a good warning that the recovering person may be about to stumble over some more of life's obstacles.

Remind your recovering person to HALT. That acronym will remind the abuser not to get too *H*ungry, too *A*ngry, too *L*onely, or too *T*ired. Overconfidence will cause the person to forget this admonition and could lead to a BUD.

Burr Under the Saddle

If you, the parents, simply can't do or say anything right, look out! Your recovering person is so touchy that no matter what is said or done, a relapse could be in the making, and *you* will get the blame! Once again, this is a guidepost that the person may be building up to drink and will want to use you or your actions as an excuse for drinking. Diffuse this attitude immediately by asking a nondefensive question such as "Sally, I'm wondering what is going on with you that makes you so irritable with me [or with what I'm doing]." Hopefully, the answer will be, "I'm not mad at you; I *really want to drink, that's all!*"

What if that's *not* the answer? What if the answer is more like, "Nothing's wrong, I'm not irritable, and I wish you'd leave me alone!" Well, then, the ball is back in your court. You have to take a stab: "I get the feeling you want a drink. What can I do to help?" Most likely, this will illicit the response you're after.

You can then proceed to help your child through this verbalization of what is really causing the irritation and general bitchiness and how you might help him or her resist this urge to drink.

Molehills

Here's a guidepost that you can really count on, almost 100 percent! When your recovering person simply acts like everything that is said or done, every chore or task that is assigned is a great big deal, look out! My grandmother used to compare this attitude to a "dog worrying a bone to death!" When a little thing becomes a monumental pyramid instead of the molehill it really is, a BUD is looming on the horizon.

Merlinism

I've always been a big King Arthur/Camelot nut, so "Merlinism" is my guidepost term for the recovering person who is constantly seeking some kind of magic in the form of a cure for drinking and, hence, alcoholism. This is the person who will always bring you the newspaper clipping about a new "sober pill," "alcoholism cure," or other magical, wonderful, wizardry of Merlin the magician that will make the alcoholism vanish! Alas, no such thing exists, at least in this day and age, and so "Merlinism" tells

101

me that the recovering peson is really building up to drink, is indulging heavily in denial, and is waiting for a magic potion to "cure" the disease.

Too High on the Hog

Grandiose behavior is a real guidepost that will help alert you to a BUD in the making. This is nothing more than a return to the old "set up the whole bar on me!" routine, except now it applies to *everything*, not just alcohol! When the recovering person is buying, buying, buying, and generally behaving like "Daddy Warbucks" in words and deeds, you can look for the next step to be "one little drink or two" as a reward for all the largesse he or she has been dispensing to others!

Living beyond one's means is a trait of the alcoholic; it's also a trait of the recovering person who is having a BUD!

Depression

This guidepost is almost too obvious, but it is many times overlooked as being a clue to wanting to drink. For the young person in particular it seems as if there can be no more sunny days without a "kegger" or two to look forward to. This depression needs to be confronted with such statements as, "I know you are down about this drinking problem. But we can lick it together, and things *will* get better!" You may take some heavy flak about your "Pollyanna" attitude, but stay with it. You reinforce your recovering person by saying, "I know you're depressed, but I also know you won't drink because of it! You're doing *so well* with your program!"

Trading Addictions

We will talk about other substances in Chapter 13, but for now, be alert for signs that your recovering person is suddenly getting hooked on other activities—people, places, and things—with the same addictive-type fervor with which the person drank. This is a sure sign that a BUD is coming. The alcoholic has a tendency to jump right into the middle of things, to do nothing in moderation, to ignore the HALT admonition, and therefore simply to trade the addiction to alcohol for an addiction to something, someone, or some other habit, hobby, or diversion! Moderation in all things is a protection against having a BUD.

Keep these twelve guideposts in mind, adding other BUD-type behaviors you and the alcohol abuser may observe.

Having a BUD is a natural part of the recovery process, and while it might seem scary for you at the beginning, you will learn to confront it and be very comfortable with it.

I have heard many nine-, ten-, and even six-year-old youngsters confront a recovering parent with "Are you having a BUD?" after the whole family has been in treatment and heard about the process of building up to drink. All family members should be aware of this possibility, and should come to understand it as a healthy part of the recovery process.

THE BENEFIT OF A RELAPSE

If the denial of the drinking problem has been there all along, then the relapse is a *good* thing! It helps cement the fact that the person in treatment has a disease that won't just go away.

The relapse then becomes an important therapeutic tool. It does for the alcoholic or alcohol-abusing person what many hours of lectures may not have done quite so effectively; it drives home the knowledge that the THIQ factor is always present, always in the ready position (like the loaded mousetrap), and will spring into action again with the first sips of alcohol—*no matter how long the person has been refraining from drinking!*

Is this *your* failure? Are you responsible for the person's returning to drinking? Of course not!

For you to own responsibility for the relapse makes as much sense as for you to own responsibility for the alcoholism in the first place. Remember, your only responsibility concerning the problem is to *do something about it,* not to take off on the guilt trip associated with the acts of drinking.

Where to go from here? You, the parents, have invested all this time (and perhaps money) in the process of getting well, and your young adult stops off "just to have one beer," and before you know it, he or she is drunk.

While it seems awfully bleak, and while it appears that you have returned to square one on this gameboard, you really have moved ahead! Now there is no reason for the alcoholic to doubt what we all know: that the alcoholic is just one drink away from the next drunk, no matter the length of his or her sobriety. You no longer have to test the system after that first relapse. It will prove itself, and your young person will have discovered it the hard way.

It becomes a step forward instead of backward because it helps reinforce this truism. It's like the loaded pistol we talked about earlier. There is no need to keep testing the possibility of the gun's discharging when you pull the trigger. If the gun is loaded, it's going to fire!

What you are going to have to guard against is your fierce anger at what has happened. You are going to have to tell yourselves over and over that your young alcoholic didn't drink to hurt you. He or she acted totally to disprove what everyone has been telling him or her, namely, "you are an alcoholic; you can't *ever* drink!"

The fact that you are hurt is your problem; you have given your young adult the power to hurt you with his or her drinking relapse. Well, what you have freely given, you can freely take away! You must tell yourselves—and, by all means, share it in your group therapy and family therapy sessions—that you are not responsible.

Say this over and over until it becomes second nature. It was not you who decided to stop after work and "see the old gang"; it was not you who decided to "have just one beer" or "only one banana daiquiri." Your child did that all on his own, and he must accept the consequences all alone.

What you can do is accept the idea that you have all just leaped over a giant hurdle, the hurdle of denial! Now it won't be necessary to waste a lot of time and effort on proving that there is an alcohol problem. It is time now to get on with the wellness process that follows a relapse.

AFTER THE RELAPSE

Here are some tools, in the form of questions to discuss as a family, that can help you understand the cause of a relapse and prevent recurrences.

1. What do you (the young abuser) think went wrong to cause the relapse?
2. What do we want to do about it?
3. What steps should we take to help prevent this from happening again?
4. What were you (the alcoholic) using as an excuse when you started to drink?
5. How much influence do you (the abuser) think your old peer group played in your decision to take that first drink?
6. What do *you* (the young adult) want to do about that (the influence of old friends)?
7. Did you (the alcoholic) even *think* about calling for help (therapist, AA sponsor, therapy peer group friends)?
8. What is *your* (the abuser's) plan for handling this if it comes up again? (Notice, we did not ask for the *parents'* plan!)
9. Do your (the abuser's) old friends know you are in treatment for alcoholism? Do they know about you and AA?
10. As a family, are we keeping all the lines of communication open and accessible?

These ten question-tools are just a sample; there are perhaps dozens more that can be used to determine a plan of action to help prevent another relapse. Remember that you are not searching for the ultimate cause of the relapse; you know that the alcoholic drinks (and drank in the relapse) because he or she has a disease that requires constant tending! Rather, you're looking for hints of day-to-day problems that may be contributing to a BUD.

The question about whether you're keeping all lines of communication open and accessible is a very important one. Very often the alcoholic will want to place the blame for the relapse on his or her inability to talk out a particular problem with you. It probably will go even further back than *talking* about a problem; even *mentioning one* sometimes is so scary as to seem like reason enough for a relapse.

That's where parents really have to do hard work! You may have to start all over to reinforce the idea that you are always available to hear a complaint, a real honest-to-God bitch about something! What you don't want is for things to get so far out of control that the alcoholic *uses* your inability to listen to those bitches as an excuse to drink! Maybe the contract terms are becoming so restrictive that your young person feels "strangled." Maybe there has been a marital problem; a work-related disaster may have cropped up. It could be *anything* that is applying pressure on your young abuser that makes him or her afraid to bring it up!

The logic of the alcoholic is really simple: "I can't tell Mom and Dad that I'm losing my job. That'll just be the straw that breaks the camel's back! If I have just one drink, maybe I can calm down enough to find a way to talk to Dad about it, though!"

Pretty obviously, the "one" drink is only the start of a relapse. Now Mom and Dad can be angry about something they already are involved with, the kid's alcohol problem! Sometimes it takes hours of therapy to uncover the hidden pressures that have been building up to drink.

When those hidden pressures finally surface, parents can

be heard to say, almost in unison, "Why didn't you *tell* us?" And why *didn't* he or she tell you? Because of fear—honest, deep-rooted fear of once again being classified as a "family failure." ("Isn't it bad enough that I've got a drinking problem? What if I lay my school troubles on Mom and Dad? They'll really have a fit over that!")

So the kid drinks. Mom and Dad can handle that! They're used to dealing with that problem. And so it goes. You can pick any other problem that's left undiscussed among family members, and if there is an alcoholic involved, you can count on his eventually using the unspoken as a reason or an excuse for drinking.

That's why the recovery process must involve the entire family. It's important for you, the parents, to be doing as much work as the young adult.

You are constantly going to face the possibility that you have made it virtually impossible for your children to communicate with you! Fear has been the ruler in too many families. The kids who are afraid to confront their parents over important (and sometimes unimportant) personal issues just learn to bury their feelings more deeply inside.

So, if you have been a party to stopping or limiting the communication process, do something about it! Go back to the basics and see where you let the communication gaps develop between you and your children. In what ways could you improve the open exchange of opinions among you?

Using the relapse as a vehicle for making changes, you can honestly admit to your alcoholic that "maybe I haven't seemed as willing to listen as before," or say, "Please tell me if you have been afraid to talk with us about [something]." It's amazing how human beings just assume that things are going along on an even keel; then a disaster of some kind strikes, and everyone stands around asking, "What happened?"

That's why I say the relapse is a step forward and not

backward; it provides a vehicle for change. It literally *cries* for change. Something has to be different than it was before, or more relapses will happen.

Not all of the changes will be ones that parents can make. Most of them will have to come from the alcoholic, with an eye to realizing that basic lifestyles will have to undergo serious examination if lifelong sobriety is going to be a possibility.

You can't pick and choose his or her friends; you *can* reemphasize the need for the alcoholic to make such an examination. How much importance is he or she willing to place on lifelong sobriety? Pass the ball firmly back to the young abuser and don't take more responsibility for the various turns in his or her life.

The tendency for failure may be so deeply ingrained in your alcoholic child that he or she just expects never to succeed in anything, including sobriety. There is nothing more pitiful than to hear a young alcoholic talk about expecting to fail. You have to reinforce the good qualities that may have become submerged in the child's eagerness to deal with the alcohol problem. You've been providing that reinforcement—either positive or negative—throughout your child's life. How many times did Junior bring home grades that were just "not quite up to par"? Whose "par"? Yours? How many times was a particular boyfriend "not acceptable," and by whose standards? Conversely, how often were minor acts overrewarded, making your alcoholic feel that he or she could *never* do anything wrong? This type of reinforcement can prevent your child from ever getting used to the idea that he just might possibly stumble once or twice in life! That helps him feed his belief that he might be able to drink sometime later in life, even though he is an alcoholic!

Somewhere in between those examples is a happy medium, a healthy medium. It is one that says, "It's OK to fail! It's OK to make a mistake or two!" What isn't OK is being closed to examining the way you are living your life. You must be willing to make whatever changes are necessary to prevent drinking relapses from happening over and over.

Psychologists tell us that we write out life scripts when we are four or five years old. That is, we are pretty much predictable by then as to how we will handle life's problems. I like to think that therapy is a way in which we can rewrite those scripts. Certainly a relapse literally *demands* a rewrite, and it is one of the methods we use in the treatment of the disease of alcoholism.

The patient is told quite bluntly that if some changes (rewrites) are not made in his or her lifestyle, then another relapse is sure to happen! What the relapse has provided is the perfect opportunity, the "executive editor" for doing those rewrites.

Alcoholics in recovery who have had a relapse invariably ask, "What happened? Am I going to keep making the same mistake?" The answer, at least from me, is, "I don't know. *Are* you?" Then I ask, "What are you going to do about it?"

The parent in me would probably like to say, "What can *I* do about it *for* you?" That's what the parent in you is going to want to say, and that will defeat the entire purpose of the rewrite. If the relapse can be looked on as a potentially positive step in the overall recovery process, it will have served a very worthwhile purpose.

Let's make something clear in our discussion of the temporary return to drinking; the *ideal* recovery program happens without ever needing a relapse. Unfortunately, alcoholism rarely reflects ideals; mostly, it confronts families with cold, hard facts! We do not build relapses into our treatment program, nor does any other program, I am sure. However, neither do we automatically throw someone out of treatment when a relapse occurs.

You will never find an AA group closing its doors to a person who has relapsed. Quite the contrary! Recovering alcoholics never give up! They never admit that there isn't another opportunity to make changes in their lives to prevent another slip from happening.

That philosophy needs to apply to you, too! You are not going to find a perfect formula for making recovery easy, long-lasting, or free from personal pain. It is a process you must go through to try to discard what doesn't work and retain the things that do.

Among the tools for reexamination and renewal after a failure (relapse) are these questions:

1. Are we still having family discussions?
2. Are we making necessary adjustments (changes) in the way we do things?
3. Are we as parents willing to rewrite some life script material of our own? (Are we still looking for perfection, for example?)
4. Have we been sticking to our contract?
5. Is our basic contract still viable? (Maybe there is new information that necessitates a rewrite.)
6. Have we been keeping our own appointments for group and individual therapy, thus setting a high-priority example?
7. Have we remembered the disease concept, preventing a new set of excuses for the relapse from cropping up?

Negative answers to these questions might be termed the "seven deadly sins" of the relapse, because they certainly seem to happen over and over. We either get lazy and drop the tools placed before us, or we never pick them up and use them at all.

There is no magical way to deal with this disease, and the only efforts that work are those you apply on a daily basis. This leads to a very important point for you to keep in the forefront of your minds: *be consistent.*

Nothing is harder for the alcoholic to deal with than double messages. If the parents are not consistent in the way they act, if they are not consistent in the consequences that are set, then the alcoholic will try to push the limits of whatever has been established. It's only human, after all, to try to get away with something.

If parents fail to treat the drinking episode in a manner that is consistent with the contract you have drawn up, then the contract isn't worth the paper it's written on! If you decided that there were some other pressures on your son or daughter that seemingly justified the slip, you are in big trouble!

What you are delivering to that person is the message that, given one set of circumstances, drinking just might be OK! ("If Marnie hadn't lost her job, the relapse wouldn't have happened!") What do you say, then, the next time, when everything has been going along just peachy-keen for Marnie and she relapses anyhow?

Are you going to get angry and start shoving the contract in her face, *at that point? Consistency* means that you treat the relapse the same way, whether it happens once or a half-dozen times. You never lose sight of the fact that alcoholism is a disease and therefore a fickle beast at best.

When parents act with consistency no double messages will be delivered. They will offer a very clear, single-purpose message:

"We love you; we care about you. The relapse happened, and it could happen again, but we want to know what you intend to do about preventing it!"

That message should never change! The emphasis clearly remains on what the alcoholic is going to do, what scripting change he or she intends to carry out. What *you* decide to do for yourselves responds directly to what the alcoholic shares with you. If family communications have broken down and have been advanced as one of the areas that may have contributed to the alcoholic's burying his or her feelings, you need to do something about it.

Remember, that doesn't mean you are accepting the breakdown of communications as the reason for the relapse; it *does* mean you are willing to reemphasize that portion of your own wellness program.

What has to be avoided at all costs is self-pity! There simply isn't any room for that in your program! You will really go back to square one if you begin the process of climbing up on that old "pity pot" and immersing yourself in a sea of old guilts and poor-me complaints.

Coupled with avoiding self-pity is the process of recognizing both the fear of failure *and* the fear of success on the part of your alcoholic. We have already discussed what the tendency to fail has meant in the relapsing process. What about fear of success? Many alcoholics are seemingly afraid to whip their disease!

That may sound strange, but it can happen. If they are successful all the time, then they have been taught and firmly believe that even more will be expected of them! We know the overachiever outperforms himself constantly, striving for perfection.

If the young alcoholic's recovery program is going along *too* smoothly, and if she possesses the drive for success, she could initiate a relapse just to make sure she is still getting the attention she deserves. "Look," she says, "I've got this alcohol thing whipped [just like everything *else* I've tackled in life]! I'll show you how well by being able to have just *one drink!"*

Deep down he or she may know that there isn't a chance in the world of quitting with just one, and his or her fear of success might just try to prove it! Suppose these youngsters *could* have just one drink and quit, then could go on for the rest of their lives having to prove one thing after another. What an awful burden! So, a relapse can settle the question, can't it?

So, as you've read in this chapter, it is possible that what you may have considered a *failure* can turn out to be a positive event. That is, a relapse isn't the end of the world, either for your alcoholic or for you. It certainly isn't a desirable occurrence, but it also isn't a sign of either weakness or more sickness than originally perceived.

Generally, you can treat the relapse as a failure in order to elicit necessary changes, initiate a rewrite of one's life scripts to ensure more solid, lifelong sobriety.

The only changes you can make, however, are *yours!* You can't be responsible for making changes for your alcoholic youngster. You can continue to drill away at the problem with the tools you have learned, keeping a positive attitude that says, "Together, we can win the battle!"

11

• • •

Go to Group;
Go Directly
to Group!

"Where am *I* supposed to go for help, Mom?"

"God! Sometimes I think I'm out there all alone!"

Abusing young people will find it very difficult to tackle their recovery problems alone; for that matter, I believe almost *anyone* can go through the recovery process much more successfully with group support. That's certainly not an original idea, as the very foundation of group therapy is the premise that you can gain valuable insight into and support for the proven ways to put alcoholism in remission by sharing your problems with others who have the same problem.

If you are all involved in a treatment program, then the group experience is already a vital part of your therapy. But you will still have to make sure that *attendance* at any group session is a very high priority. It won't do a bit of good if your young person always finds something else he or she has to do in the time slot that group has been scheduled for. You will have to bear down, particularly as the treatment program progresses and when it looks like a long, slow process.

I can't begin to tell you how many people have told our staff that, if it weren't for their group, they wouldn't have a chance of staying sober! And that's good news! It is the very pulse of the AA program that says quite simply to anyone, "If I can do it [stay sober], so can you!"

Most young people enter their period of recovery thinking that they are absolutely unique, that there just *couldn't* be anyone else with the same pressures to drink that they have! That's perfectly OK and normal. The alcohol abuser has been told for so long by so many people that getting well is just a matter of "putting your mind to it" that she begins to feel she is some kind of mental incompetent, particularly when failure stares at her from the bathroom mirror morning after morning!

So, it's perfectly natural for an abuser to believe that he must be *unique* in having a drinking problem. Of course he is not unique at all, and his first group experience quickly confirms that. I have worked with some very hostile young people, and it's always gratifying to hear them talk about their first night with their small therapy group.

"It was kinda interesting," they say, "Seems like the guy that works for that computer store goes crazy like I do!"

"What makes that strange to you?" asks the therapist.

"Well, he seems so educated; me, I only got through high school."

"Sounds like you think he has enough education to whip his problem, and you don't. Is that it?" the therapist continues.

"Yeah, I guess so. Yet you've been telling me that education or willpower has nothing to do with it. I've got a disease, right?"

"Well, it seems like he has the same fight you're having. So what does that say to you?" the therapist might go on.

So it goes through the session, reinforcing the fact that all members of the small group share a common problem, alcoholism or alcohol abuse, without regard to race, color, creed, education, position, or any other demographic factor. The common enemy is alcohol, and, as the old saying goes, there's definitely "strength in numbers."

But let's get back to the original question posed at the beginning. Suppose there is no group program in your treatment setup. Then the answer needs to be found in AA. In Alcoholics Anonymous there is a group for every imaginable category.

Your young person can be involved in a straight closed group, which is limited to recovering people. He or she can even get more closely allied with a group of young recovering people. It will take some effort to locate just the right group, and that can only bring good results. It means your young abuser will have to go to some meetings and assert himself to find out where there might be a group better suited to him.

Usually the "hotline" of AA, listed in the "Community Service Numbers" of your telephone directory, is the primary source for finding the proper group. It's a twenty-four-hour answering service, so there can be no excuse for not getting help when you need it!

But it's a wonderful experience for your young person to go or be taken to an AA meeting by a sponsor or another friend, see other people in the same age category, and get some new bearings. But since this is a book for parents, my interest is in getting *you* involved in the group process.

So, we are looking for an AA group that is open. In an open group you can accompany your young person and take the opportunity to be very supportive. The Al-Anon experience (you can find the location of Al-Anon groups with the help of your telephone directory) will be invaluable to you. Recovering people can also attend Al-Anon meetings, but generally Al-Anon is for the wives, husbands, parents, and friends of the recovering alcoholic.

The important point to remember is that your young

person *needs* group support. She *needs* to know that she is not alone and that there are many others right in the community who are willing and anxious to help.

Earlier, I mentioned a sponsor. This is a person with AA experience who agrees to be just that—a sponsor while you begin your program of recovery. The sponsor will be available to talk with your young adult at times other than regular meeting times. They will possibly get together for lunch or for coffee. They might go to a movie together. But the most important role of a sponsor will be to see that your young person gets to meetings!

The more the alcoholic is with other people who are trying to whip the disease, the stronger he becomes.

In the open and closed meetings there are further breakdowns that will assist you in finding the group that meets your needs best.

A speaker's meeting (either open or closed) generally features one speaker for the entire hour of the meeting, though sometimes two or perhaps three invited persons will speak. This is common, particularly when an AA member is celebrating an anniversary of sobriety and has asked close friends to help with the occasion by speaking at the particular meeting at which the celebration will occur.

A discussion meeting can be open or closed. The chairperson throws the topic for the hour open to participation by all who care to say something. These meetings sometimes seem scary to newly recovering alcoholics, because they think there will be a lot of pressure on them to say something. Nothing could be further from the truth! If they are called upon to speak at a discussion meeting, they, or you, can simply say, "I think I'd rather just listen, thank you." Your wishes will be respected absolutely. There's no pressure to talk, though the *sharing* of your feelings is what recovery is all about!

The third general category of AA and Al-Anon meetings is a step meeting, which can also be open or closed. These meetings are devoted to the more complete study of one of the twelve steps of Alcoholics Anonymous or of Al-Anon. If your young person has acquired a sponsor, then the sponsor will probably be the best judge of when and where to introduce such meetings into the schedule.

If treatment at a center has been used, then I strongly urge you to investigate whatever aftercare programs are available when treatment, or at least the formal part of treatment, has been completed. Many times, a combination of formal aftercare treatment and AA is called for. Certainly AA will be the lifelong answer to sobriety, since it is available in every city in the country (and over most of the world!) on a twenty-four-hour-a-day basis.

The young person, if married, attends an AA couple group, which is in the open category, so the nonrecovering spouse can also attend. These meetings are held weekly at our treatment center, where the recovering young persons already have a sense of familiarity and where their comfort level is already high.

For the single person there are daily meetings, both open and closed, held at the center.

You will find that your local hospitals and treatment centers will most generally be involved in providing a meeting place for recovering alcoholics. Hospitals that use the AA program as part of their model of treatment will, of course, have many meetings, many times during the week.

Outpatient programs such as ours at Gateway do not have the daily contact with patients that a hospital has, so the need for more regular attendance at the treatment center becomes apparent. Thus, we use the open couples' and parents' groups as a means of providing more contact than would normally be available.

Peer group support is definitely available for all ages. If you have younger family members than the recovering person, they can get help through Ala-Teen or even Ala-Tot programs. They can and should participate in whatever family care programs are offered at the treatment center you are attending.

You may think that your five- or six- or seven-year-old youngster doesn't know anything about the alcohol problem in your family. Wrong! Over and over again, we see parents who are absolutely amazed at how much their youngsters *really know* about what's been going on and, even more, what enormous effects on their lives such a thing is having!

It's always a pleasure, really, to have a little five-year-old sitting in our office, telling us that "Daddy doesn't drink beer anymore!" Usually, the parents are astounded to hear that statement because they have deluded themselves into thinking they have masked or hidden the alcohol problems from the youngsters in the family.

It works exactly the same way if an older brother or sister is the afflicted party. Don't kid yourselves as parents by thinking you have successfully isolated the family drinker from everyone else. You haven't!

It's a serious disservice to the others in the family for you to be thinking like that. As I have "preached" over and over in this book, alcoholism is a family disease, and therefore the entire family must be included in treatment.

The importance of group therapy in aftercare becomes even more apparent as time wears on and the idea of staying in treatment becomes a heavy load, financially and emotionally. Remember, though, that there are no set rules for the length of treatment. There is no guarantee in this alcoholism business, and you all have to have it firmly and indelibly etched on your brains that recovery is a lifelong process! There is no shortcut that I know of, and there's certainly no substitute for staying in touch with other recovering alcoholics.

So many times, particularly after a relapse occurs, the recovering young abuser will admit that he has been letting his group work slide. He has allowed other things to take priority over making their meetings. Before he knows it, he has fallen back into the old ways; he is back with the *old* peer group instead of the group in which he belongs and with whom he has shared so much.

A young man I have worked with for more than two

years freely admits that it is his aftercare group that keeps his sobriety intact. He continues to attend a formal therapy group of single young adults once a week and makes his AA meetings at least three times a week.

When traveling, instead of sitting around his hotel room, this young alcoholic gets on the telephone and calls AA. He finds a meeting to his liking, and that's where he spends his time.

As parents, you will need ongoing support as well. What makes you think that there is a time limit on *your* recovery any more than on the abuser's? You will need to continue to put effort *for yourself* into this program, or you can count on making the same mistakes over and over!

So often, I hear parents tell group members about getting too comfortable with their own attitudes and that, sure enough, they find themselves repeating the old enabling patterns of the past. They find themselves going on more guilt trips than ever and realize, again, the importance of staying well by doing their group work.

I am well aware of what you are thinking right now! "Oh, sure! Easy for him to tell us of all the time we have to spend! That's his job!"

Well, you're right! It *is* my job as a therapist; but, as a recovering alcoholic and a parent, I know the truth of the "time-in, time-well" idea. The more time you put into your own program, the more time you can enjoy yourselves as "well" parents, as a well family.

If you are overly concerned about applying all this effort, just think of the time you have been spending, maybe even now, dealing with the actively drinking alcoholic in your family. How many hours have you been spending sitting in your own "bay windows" waiting for the inevitable?

As to expense, how much money has been pumped into court fines, lawyers, and automobile repair bills?

The amounts will be staggering to you if you have the courage to sit down and add them up! Of course treatment can be expensive. But once again, remember that there are public treatment programs that are based on your ability to pay, as well as private centers. So you have no excuses there.

As to the time investment, I often wonder how it would compare to the hours of bitter anguish you have "enjoyed" over the drinking of your young son or daughter. How many times do you think you would like to repeat the scenes of watching him lurch about your living room, banging off the furniture as he tries to find his way to his room after a night of drinking?

For the young abuser, the questions are just as easily posed. How many more times do you want to experience a blackout in which you don't remember where you were, what you did, or whom you were with? These are questions that you as parents should put to your abuser to counter the questions posed at the beginning of this chapter.

Your answers to those questions should be forceful and direct. You can give the support to your young person as you get support for yourself by participating in aftercare programs that are offered by your treatment center (public or private) and through the many AA programs available.

You can go with your young adult to his or her AA meetings; it is not enabling for you to help your child get to a meeting!

You can reinforce the fact that while she may *think* she is going through this disease all alone, in truth she has a veritable battalion of support from you, the parents!

If you have been the kind of parent(s) that I think you are, then you really *want* to offer support to your young abuser. It is no sign of weakness to be seen going to meetings with him; rather, it is a show of family solidarity. It is a badge of courage that every family member can wear proudly— much more proudly than when making excuses for drunken behavior and making time for more court appearances!

If you were to devise a board game of recovery, imagine that you would be moving the playing pieces around as ordered by the roll of the dice. At certain places you would land on a square that would tell you, "Take two paces forward for nonenabling." You might hit a new square that says, "Take five steps forward for getting off the guilt trip!"

You might then roll a number that lands you on a square marked "discouragement—you're playing old tapes again!" Maybe things between you and your abuser have just plain fallen apart. So you reach over into the pile of "penalty cards" on our mythical board game.

You're sure to draw the card marked, "Go to group; go *directly* to group!"

If it were my game, if I were the inventor, there would be no other cards available from which to choose! Such is my belief in the power of the group therapy process, whether treatment-oriented or AA, that I would have stacked the deck!

Go and stack your own deck of wellness, parents!

12
• • •
Getting Help
When Help
Isn't Wanted

"Who told you I *wanted* to quit drinking?"

"Why don't you just mind your own damn business!"

"I'll quit when I'm damn good and ready, not before!"

So you sit there, dumbfounded and bewildered. You're hurt and *very* angry. Why wouldn't your child want help for a drinking problem? Over and over parents torment themselves, feeling there must be some way to get help for the son or daughter they love so much. There must be some way to make that son *see* what he is doing to his life; to make that daughter realize that alcohol has taken over and that she is becoming a slave to a chemical.

Yet, the angry young person before you is demanding that you "get the hell out of my life!" The "leave me alone" and "I can take care of it without you" syndrome is one of the most frustrating to confront you. But there is a way; those who love and care for the alcoholic can make another supreme effort, even when help is not wanted by the victim.

It's called *crisis intervention* or simply *intervention*. Dr. Vernon Johnson and his superb staff at the Johnson Institute in Minneapolis pioneered this method of treatment for alcoholics. Many other practitioners, including my friend Ty Owens, have made this technique an even more effective tool.

It has been my good fortune to have trained in crisis intervention with Ty, a private practitioner in Denver. Over the years it has been possible for me to be the intervenor in a number of cases, so the techniques and the methods that I describe in this chapter are a combination of the best of the procedures that I have been able to employ in our own practice at Gateway Treatment Center.

To begin with, it's essential to understand fully that intervention is a last-ditch effort, something to be used only when all other avenues have been exhausted. The possibility of failure in "doing an intervention" is always fifty-fifty at best.

The problem with an intervention is that, if it fails, you may have lost the opportunity to approach the alcoholic with the idea of getting help for quite some time. You will have used "all your horses" and there won't be many selling points to get the alcoholic into treatment of one kind or another.

I want to stress that treatment should include getting the alcoholic into the fellowship of AA, not just formalized treatment programs. In most cases that require intervention, however, the alcoholic is probably sick enough to require hospitalization and/or outpatient treatment.

Some of the most effective intervenors are the members of AA who respond to a call for help from a family member. They will wait, if possible, for the alcoholic to *ask* for help, and then they will move with great speed and loving care to respond.

For our purposes, however, let's deal with the assumption that you will need treatment—hospital, residential (such as a halfway house), or outpatient—for your young adult who is in trouble with alcohol. In any case, participation in the fellowship of AA is an essential part of the aftercare and the best method known for maintaining lifelong sobriety!

My personal belief, and that shared by my Gateway colleagues, is that you must first *treat* the disease of alcoholism and then make every effort possible to channel the person in recovery into the AA mainstream. Many programs, both inpatient and residential as well as outpatient, will use the AA program as part of the initial treatment model.

Some, like our Gateway Treatment Center, prefer to introduce the AA program in the later stages of treatment, after an understanding of the nature and treatment of the disease has been thoroughly inculcated into the everyday living patterns of the alcoholic.

At any rate, the purpose of intervention is to get help for the person who doesn't want help! So how to begin? It will be helpful to make a list of the steps the intervention will include and then look at a typical intervention through a hypothetical scenario to show how it can work and how it can backfire.

These are the general steps I use for intervention:
1. Exploration
2. Education
3. Consequences
4. Rehearsal
5. Final Dress Rehearsal
6. Intervention
7. Family Follow-Up

An intervention calls into play professionals, family members, friends, coworkers, and employers, working in a concentrated setting of love, care, and concern, to forcefully guide the alcoholic into seeking treatment.

In my opinion, an intervention works only when the consequences set up by those involved are so firm that the alcoholic is fearful of what he or she will lose if treatment is not sought. You'll get the drift as you read through this chapter. For now, let's review the process step by step.

THE EXPLORATION

Quite simply, this step is taken when someone who cares has had to make contact with a professional or has been referred to such a person or place in the hope of getting help for someone who doesn't want it. What is required now is for those interested parties to get together and explore the ways and means of the intervention.

Remember, the "victim" is not aware of what you are thinking of doing! The element of surprise is one of the most successful "weapons" of an intervention; any hints that something is afoot will defuse the intervention, removing most or all of its impact.

It's time to state emphatically that an intervention is *not* an act of cruelty! It is an honest, forthright, and meaningful expression of love for the sick individual. You are not making this critical maneuver because you hate, but because you love! Armed with that understanding, the professional you have consulted will want to gather the immediate family members together for an exploratory talk. Some of the questions that will be posed in this first meeting should be:

1. Who will be involved?
2. Where will the intervention be held?
3. Where will the person enter treatment (in-hospital, residential, or outpatient)?
4. How will the subject be brought or "lured" to the intervention?
5. Is intervention the only option that is left?

I stress the last point because I feel strongly that when a family tries an intervention and it fails, long-term discouragement and setbacks set in and become very hard to overcome. That's why, in the exploration stage, all parties involved should be urged to give their views; all of the doubts and the fears should be expressed at this first meeting.

Fears? You bet! An intervention is a scary thing for most families, because *it may not be successful!* The people who will be involved will feel like they are all back at square one in dealing with the alcoholic. Let's put that fear aside and discuss it after looking at the other steps.

The selection of the kind of treatment program to be the target for the intervention will depend on the assessment made by the professionals you are working with. They will listen to stories of the behavior of the alcoholic or alcohol abuser, the kinds of difficulties that have resulted from the alcoholic behavior, and the possible physical characteristics and problems that might be a part of the picture.

Whether treatment will be sought as an inpatient or outpatient, for example, will be determined largely by evaluating which is likely to be more successful. Will your alcoholic be better off being removed from his or her environment and admitted to a hospital for a period of time, or will he or she be able to function in an outpatient setting, maintaining job, school, or other activities while obtaining treatment?

The selection of a residential program will also be the focus of the professional staff with whom you are working. Just believe this: The object of an intervention is to get help for someone who doesn't want it, and the professionals will want that person to enter the program or facility that they believe has the best chance of working for him or her!

Those of us who provide intervention services certainly do not make the selection of our own facility a necessary ingredient for performing the intervention. Quite the contrary! Many times I have been involved in performing the intervention for a family in which the objective was to get their loved one into a hospital or residential facility the family chose.

Cost of treatment programs vary, and the professional will help you find the ones that fit your means, including the sliding-scale (ability-to-pay) and public programs.

The site of the intervention is extremely important. The general rule should be to avoid all "safe grounds," where the alcoholic could bolt from the session and seek safety in his or her own room. Usually, a friend's or neighbor's house, a sibling's residence, or perhaps a church setting will be chosen as the place for the intervention.

Once the place has been determined, how is the lure to work? No one is going to be invited just to come and hear how he needs to be whisked off to treatment, so some sort of subterfuge is, unfortunately, necessary. This is where many family members bog down in the intervention process. They feel as if they are part of a "Judas act," a betrayal of the one they love.

When you talk about "luring" the person to the intervention, what you are really discussing is *how* to get the person to the place. Usually, a family member will suggest something that will give the professional a clue to explore further with you. It may be a birthday party or celebration of some other kind, which the alcoholic would be expected to attend anyhow. It obviously would *not* be the *alcoholic's* birthday, but rather that of another family member or friend.

Pretexts of needing repair work done, helping with a specific chore, or seeing a new movie on television are some of the other methods that can be used to help lure the person to his or her own intervention.

Now the question of who will be involved draws our attention. You have a place, a facility for treatment, and a method of getting the person to the intervention. The people who are to be actually involved are, of course, principal to the success of an intervention.

Should all the brothers and sisters, the grandparents, uncles and aunts, cousins, etc., be involved? Probably not! It's too unwieldy and too dangerous because of the heavy emotional trip that an intervention involves.

Uppermost in the selection process should be the family and friends who are (1) the people of greatest influence on the alcoholic's life and (2) the people who have the strongest consequences to impose.

Grandma and Grandpa may be very important, but they may not carry as much clout as, say, a younger brother or sister who is being more directly affected by the alcoholic's behavior. Get the idea? That's why this exploration session is held, to be able to sort the methods, the people, and the ways that will help ensure the best chance for success of the intervention. I find six to nine persons, plus the interventionist best. Other professionals will have their own criteria and will make them known to you.

An employer who will have direct effect on the livelihood of the alcoholic and who is *aware of and supportive* of treatment for the alcoholic is a valuable member of the intervention team. Close and supportive friends need to be considered and accepted or rejected, all with the same eye to their *sphere of influence* and the *strength of their consequence.* Thus, a sweetheart who will threaten to end the relationship if treatment is not sought by the alcoholic is an obviously stronger choice than a younger sibling who says, "You can't borrow my things anymore." (This may be the sibling's strongest consequence, but it's basically ineffective.)

The exploration session may contain many elements other than the ones discussed so far. Each case is specific and will breed its own set of problems. Your professional interventionist will help you talk out your fears and concerns.

You may have wondered about my continued use of the terms *professional* and *interventionist.* You *must* use a trained person to do this job! The amateur—the colleague or well-meaning doctor, the pastor or other family friend— who is not specifically and specially trained for intervention can cause a great deal of damage!

You are playing with human emotions that involve not just the alcoholic but everyone who is participating in the intervention, and trusting that process to the untrained is simply a very bad, very dangerous, and explosive decision.

THE EDUCATION

In this step you should be shown a film or videotape of a dramatized intervention and perhaps given some very basic education about what the disease is doing to the family as well as to the alcoholic. The education session will also probably focus on weeding out some of the original people who were slated to take part. Many times, after viewing or hearing about an intervention, some individuals decide not to participate, or it becomes very clear to everyone else that those people should not participate.

For example, daughters or sons (in older-adult interventions) who simply can't bring themselves to "turn against" Mom or Dad, often eliminate themselves from the intervention. The more powerful the educational presentation, the more likely it is that you may lose some of these people. This is the point at which it *should* happen; don't wait for the actual intervention to find out that someone can't go on with his or her role.

Whatever the education that is planned for the people who have been selected initially, it will be this session that will lead to the next step.

THE CONSEQUENCES

This is, at first sight, a difficult step. The consequences here are the kinds of appropriate action that people can take or threaten to take if the alcohol abuser refuses help. Remember, the example of the younger sibling's refusal to lend her belongings is not a very good consequence.

At this stage the interventionist asks each member of the team to make a list of alcohol-related incidents involving the subject of the intervention and the team member. This list cannot be made at this session; it's something everyone needs to think about alone and be prepared to bring to the first rehearsal.

Along with that list (sometimes called the *indictments*) are specific things that each individual is willing to say he or she will do, *if* the subject refuses to seek help.

In the cases of individuals seeking to get alcoholic spouses into treatment, the most powerful weapon of consequence is the threat of divorce. The key, of course, is that the spouse *must be determined to carry out the threat!*

It's totally ineffective for you to bring in a list of consequences that you have no intention of carrying out! As parents, your most powerful consequence is probably to tighten the financial screws to the maximum. A typical example might be a father telling his son in intervention that, unless the son gets help, *all* financial help he has been providing will stop.

Suppose a traffic citation (DUI—Driving Under the Influence) has been issued as a result of an alcoholic incident; the resultant loss of the use of other family vehicles then becomes a good consequence. Other brothers or sisters can refuse to drive or lend their cars to the offender unless the offender seeks help. Get the idea?

An employer has the best shot at putting his consequences where his mouth is. "If you don't get help, Larry, I'm going to suspend [or fire] you. You're one of my best employees, but I can't see you continuing with us in the condition you're in!"

Even the youngest members of the family who are going to participate in the intervention can offer consequences, and, in fact, these are sometimes the most touching. I recall one little guy, just seven years old, who tearfully told his older alcohol-abusing brother that if he didn't "go to get help," he wouldn't "ever let you work on my stamp collection again!" It didn't seem like much, but the way the child brought it off in his own halting, whispery voice was a real gut-wrencher and helped turn the trick!

Once again, the most important element of the consequences is that nothing can be used or stated as a consequence that the person is not absolutely prepared to carry out! All of the teeth are pulled from a consequence when it is never brought into play. In the case of a mate threatening divorce, I will not proceed with an intervention until the mate has actually seen or contacted a lawyer or at least can show a standard petition form for dissolution of marriage. If he or she can produce some kind of evidence of serious intent, then the consequence is allowed.

Such actions can always be put on hold; most attorneys who are aware of the circumstances will know and understand the reasoning for using such a powerful weapon. I have used a family attorney as a member of the intervention to present a consequence to a young adult male being forcefully guided into treatment.

The attorney was there to represent with forceful action the consequence delivered by a grandmother who was unable to attend the intervention due to illness. The attorney read a letter from the grandmother instructing him to "substantially alter her bequest" to the young man, should he refuse to "straighten out his life and give up drink." The young man loved his grandmother very much; she had raised him for most of his life, and it was a powerful consequence. It wasn't just the potential loss of money from her, but the scathing attack of the letter delivered (through an attorney) that helped turn the tide toward treatment.

Members of the intervention team should *not* share what their consequences are until the next step of the process, the rehearsal.

THE REHEARSAL

At this meeting all are assembled in a room the interventionist has made available, usually not the actual room where the intervention will take place. The members of the group are seated in a semi-circle facing two chairs. One of those chairs is for the interventionist, and the other is for the subject of the intervention.

Since this is a rehearsal, obviously the subject is not present; the empty chair just represents the subject. One at a time, the individual members of the intervention team read from their prepared lists. Each list should be headed with the phrase, "Larry [or whomever], I *love you* and I *care about you!*" This phrase is used by everyone in his or her turn. It should be underlined and is *absolutely* the first thing that is said by each person.

The person speaking then continues by giving specific *alcohol-related incidents of behavior* in which the person and the subject were involved. Give specific times, dates, and places. For example, Mother says, "Larry, last week when my bridge group was here you came into the room.

The smell of beer on your breath was overpowering, and I was *humiliated!* You were obviously drunk, and it was only three in the afternoon!" Or, from a younger brother: "Larry, when my friend Jeff came to spend the night Saturday, you came into our room and started messing up our Monopoly game! You were drunk, and I was ashamed of you!"

You get the idea. But each speaker begins with the "love you/ care about you" phrase. One by one, each speaker gives his list of "grievances," being careful that they are all alcohol-related and documented by specific time, date, and place. At the conclusion of the list of each person's griev-ances, the consequence is given.

The interventionist will suggest that each person of the group closely watch the member who is speaking. This focuses the attention on what's being said. It will be *hard* on you. You will hear things from your own group that you never knew, perhaps, and it will bring tears of hurt and anguish! This is the reason for the rehearsal. It lets you get the surprises out in the open; it lets you deal with the enormity of what you are about to do, namely, share feelings openly!

No matter what happens, *no matter how hard it is,* no member of the group should get up or go to the person speaking when that person falters, cries, or otherwise falls apart while giving his or her grievances/consequence list. The interventionist will stress this, but you need to be prepared. You will want to go to the person who is crying or sobbing, but you must not! A large part of the effectiveness of the intervention lies in the fact that *all* group members become aware of what the subject's alcoholic behavior has done to each member of this group who loves the alcoholic!

You will be guided by whatever educational session materials you have used and by your interventionist in other fine details to be worked out in the rehearsal.

THE FINAL DRESS REHEARSAL

For the final dress rehearsal you will probably be in the actual place in which the intervention is to be staged. Your lists have been pared down, with some items added or eliminated, and some people may have been eliminated since the first rehearsal because of either their inability to deliver their consequences or the lack of strength behind their consequences.

In the final dress rehearsal all details of how the subject will be controlled are carefully explained by the interventionist. He or she will have some prepared, memorized script to use for this purpose. Here's what I use:

"Larry, your family and your friends are here today because they love you and they care about you. I want you to sit here with me and listen to what they have to say. I don't want you to interrupt, but I'll give you a chance to speak later!"

That's just an idea of the general tone an interventionist might use to get things rolling. Each person has his or her own way of doing things, but you get the drift of how it will sound. The sixth step of the process is the actual intervention.

THE INTERVENTION

Now the rehearsal, the questioning, the doubts, the fears and anxieties come into focus. This "D-Day" is critical, emotional, and utterly draining! This is it! The intervention itself will probably take an hour. The subject has been "duped," by whatever means, into walking or being led into a roomful of people.

The group has already been assembled, in their chairs, in their proper order of speaking. This order of speaking has been worked out in your rehearsals and is designed to be the most effective sequence. Let me assure you that this setting has a powerful *shock value* for the subject the moment he or she enters that room!

I never fail to be amazed at the element of surprise that works for us! The alcoholic doesn't immediately understand or comprehend what is happening. The subject thought he was coming to a particular function or party or whatever has been used as the "bait" and suddenly finds himself in a room with family, friends, employer, sweetheart, pastor, and a stranger who is telling him, basically, to "sit down and be quiet and listen to what these people have to say!"

It's mind-boggling! It's one of the reasons that intervention has to be carefully planned, thought about, rehearsed, and staged for maximum effectiveness! The pure emotion of the event is swept through the room like a powerful gale, and only hearing the statement "We love you and we care about you!" over and over reassures the entire group that what they are doing is not cruel but loving, caring, and concerned. This intervention will be difficult, so don't treat it lightly. It is, nonetheless, a very effective tool *when all other means have been tried and have failed.*

Just as in the rehearsal, it is of paramount importance that you avoid leaving your chair and running into the arms of the subject! The subject may burst into tears while he or she listens to the alcoholic incidents that have touched the family member or friend reciting them; he or she may cry out of sheer empathy at seeing a brother, a sister, parent, or sweetheart sitting there sobbing while pouring out their grievances and consequences.

However, at no time must the subject be allowed contact with any group member until he or she has agreed to enter treatment. The interventionist will gently restrain the subject from leaving his chair; *you* will have to restrain yourselves!

When all the group has been heard from, the interventionist will tell the subject what his or her choices are: enter the treatment selected or face the consequences that this roomful of people have given.

THE FAMILY FOLLOW-UP

Finally, we get to the last section of this process, the family follow-up. It's important that, *regardless* of the outcome of the intervention, the family members who have participated in the intervention get a chance to deal with their feelings. Some very heavy emotions have been expressed in the hour of the intervention. Even if the subject has refused treatment, the family members need the opportunity to deal with their feelings.

The Unsuccessful Intervention

For a moment, let's talk about the repercussions of an unsuccessful intervention. Suppose the subject simply said, "To hell with all of you!" and stalked angrily from the room. Has the intervention been a failure? In some ways, yes; in others, no.

The immediate failure is obvious; the subject has not agreed to enter treatment, at least for the moment. This does not mean that he or she will *always* refuse treatment, but for now, the refusal has been stated clearly.

If the subject gets up and leaves the room, *no one* must try to stop him! Nor should anyone make any other move, except to let him or her go. You are dealing with an angry, hurt, confused person at this stage, one who feels the whole world is against him because of his drinking!

For the moment, it is the family members left sitting in that room who need immediate help. I try to schedule appointments for individual, conjoint, and family therapy sessions as soon as possible after a "failed" intervention.

A family session of at least one hour should take place *right then and there,* just to give the people in that room the opportunity to deal with what has just happened and with the apparent failure of the plan everyone has worked on for so many hours.

Most interventionists will have arranged for individual family members to be seen for a session or two, assuming the family is not going to enter treatment along with the abuser. If such arrangements have not been made, *insist* on them. Once the heavy emotions have been opened up, they must be dealt with, even if the alcoholic chooses to do nothing for himself or herself.

Now let's look back at the alcoholic who bolted out of the

room. If he or she has chosen to do nothing for his or her alcohol problem, must you give up? Can you have someone "put" into treatment? Not really. There is a common misconception that parents or anyone else can just put someone into treatment whether they want to go or not. Well, this is a good news/bad news kind of situation. In most states, a court order to *hold and treat* an alcoholic can be secured with the assistance of a physician, or perhaps an officer of the court. That's the good news. But the bad news is that "hold and treat" is good for just twenty-four hours, or perhaps two or three days of de-toxification.

In many situations, a patient will enter a hospital or other facility for treatment, only later to sign himself out of the place! The staff will try their darndest to keep him there, but if the patient really wants to go and is capable of doing so, you probably can't stop him! The paperwork will indicate the patient left treatment "AMA" or "against medical advice," but he can leave, nonetheless.

This chapter has given you a rough outline of what an intervention is all about. The fine tuning simply cannot be done within these pages; it's too complex and too variable with each individual situation. All you need to know is that this is a very powerful tool in the projected treatment of the alcoholic, a tool that can turn lives around and can spell the difference between hope and despair!

But, like all tools, it must be used very carefully. Placed in the wrong or inexperienced hands, it can be harmful—almost, I believe, to the point of disrepair. Seek *professional* help! Spend the time necessary to make sure that an intervention is what is needed and to investigate all other available avenues thoroughly to get your loved one into treatment. Remember, no matter what you do, it is through love and care that you act!

13
• • •
Booze by
Any Other Name

"So what's wrong if I smoke a little dope? I'm giving up booze, aren't I?"

"Hey, man! I can *handle* a snort or two of coke! It's beer that gets me where it hurts!"

These are typical responses given by the young (or older) abuser who wants to trade one substance for another. "Take away my alcohol, but let me keep my pot!" Doesn't that seem like a fair trade? After all, marijuana smoking *couldn't* be as bad as getting drunk!

All the news today tells us that cocaine is "turning on middle-class America." The "in" party thing, particularly among celebrities, is to have a dish of coke and lovely silver spoons right on the dinner table for your guests. So what's the big deal?

Well, simply stated, when the alcoholic trades his alcohol for another substance such as marijuana or cocaine, he historically returns to the use of his substance of choice. If that substance is alcohol, then an abuser will inevitably return to drinking.

The alcoholic will kid herself for a while, believing that she is "handling" the high that is being obtained from another drug, but very quickly that high isn't good enough; it doesn't provide enough "kick," nor does the kick last long enough.

One of the most widely abused of these alternate drugs is Valium. Well-meaning, but perhaps not alcohol-trained, physicians freely prescribe Valium or Librium as a means of helping "control the nerves" while a person is trying to give up alcohol. You might just as well be giving that person dried vodka!

Both Valium and Librium, and a host of other drugs that fall into the sedative class, simply replace alcohol. The alcoholic doesn't have to drink; he or she simply goes around in a state of Valium sedation, exactly as if he or she had never given up alcohol in the first place!

In all fairness to the physician, he or she may have been deliberately lied to by the patient as to the severity of the alcohol problem, the amount taken each day, and so forth. The well-meaning doctor treats what he sees before him and wishes to provide some relief from the "anxiety" his patient has presented.

It's a shame! So many times a patient enters treatment for alcoholism and then thinks it's OK to form a daily pot, coke, or Valium habit "just to help me get through this!" Your young person will probably want to try the same thing.

Parents need to be aware that this is simply *not acceptable*. The treatment of alcoholism and alcohol abuse calls for the person in treatment to be absolutely *substance-free*, and that includes a whole array of popular drugs.

Certainly the idea of getting help for the alcohol problem does not accept trading the booze for anything else that allows a person to go through life stoned, unable to deal with the simplest of problems. And your young people can be tricky!

It's always amazing to hear parents tell others in their group how they "had no idea" that their child was using pot or snorting coke! They seemed absolutely dumbfounded that they could all be going through treatment for a disease like alcoholism and then have a *new* drug problem crop up!

And how is this other substance use discovered? Usually, the alcoholics themselves come clean to their therapist or to their own therapy group. Because confidentiality is respected and guarded in a group or at an individual session, the parents very often are the last to know, if indeed they ever know.

Many times, particularly when parents are paying for treatment, there will be little choice but to disclose this new drug abuse. The young person will probably have signed a disclosure statement that allows his or her parents access to certain pieces of information while in treatment.

Just as often, however, the young adult has said, "No way!" to disclosing *anything* about his treatment progress. This request should be honored completely, no matter how much pressure may be applied by the parents, spouse, or anyone else concerned with the patient.

So how do you find out that your kid has been "doing real well" in the alcohol department but actually has been smoking marijuana joints on a regular basis? It may sound impossible to you, but eventually *most* patients do admit to this additional substance abuse. There is something about the bonding of individuals in groups that creates a very strong desire to help each other. Indeed, this is a major element in group therapy. It is a principal reason for the success of AA. The fact that there are others who care about you and your problems and who stand ready to help can give the alcoholic and family much-needed strength.

It's very hard for a person to sit in a small group therapy session, hear some other member of the group disclose a setback or a relapse, and then act like "Snow White." The pressure to reveal other substance use comes *from within*, and it's not very long before the young person is willing to tell his parents as well.

139

So the parents become temporarily devastated. They say they have put "all this time and effort" into treatment, only to find out that their recovering child is using drugs. Handling this problem boils down to a combination of education and motivation.

Education requires both you and the recovering person to understand the nature of alcoholism, which almost guarantees that the person will return to drinking if he keeps using other substances. And he'll be drinking more than he did before.

Well, that's a good feeling, isn't it? Wouldn't we all like to have the ability to take something that would help us through life? Sure we would! So what would make you think that, when you take such a substance (alcohol) away from your young person, he is not going to try to *replace* it?

Alcoholics turn more and more to drink in an effort *to avoid coping with life*, though they all delude themselves into thinking that the reason they need alcohol is to cope! The real coping comes with sobriety; that's when the person who has been chemically dependent really begins to face up to his life and learn the ways he must change his thoughts and actions in order to survive without alcohol.

The second element, motivation, is an elusive tool that comes largely from within. Even though the pressure of group, or the internal family pressure, or perhaps a pending legal or court issue may be an *outward* reason for the person disclosing other substance use, most of the motivation for becoming chemically free is personal.

No one likes to fail; it is particularly abhorrent to young people who have probably spent most of their lives trying to excel. Being caught up in a merry-go-round of trading alcohol for pot, coke, or speed (amphetamines) finally gets to them. They are failing at whipping their problem, and they are seeing and being with others like themselves who *are* winning the battle! So they 'fess up!

You don't have to be devastated or disappointed by the disclosure of other drug abuse. Your young people have spent a lot of time, energy, and money (maybe a lot of yours!) getting sick. Aren't they (and you) entitled to at least an equal amount of time to get well?

So, instead of getting all bent out of shape over this new development, let's look at some ways you can learn to deal with it. For one thing, it *must be confronted.* Don't think for a minute the alcoholic's use of another substance is going to go away, any more than the alcohol problem has. Treat both as a threat to recovery. The sooner you can say to your recovering alcoholic, "Look, Ted, I know you've been smoking pot! Let's talk," the better off you both will be. Nothing, absolutely *nothing,* is to be gained from ignoring the facts. If your son or daughter has divulged other substance use on his or her own, here are some lines of inquiry for you to use as you *sit down together to talk.*

1. How long has this been going on?
2. What do you want to do about it?
3. What can we do to help you with this?
4. What's your *real* commitment to treatment?
5. Does your therapist (counselor) know?
6. Have you told your friends you're in treatment?
7. Do you still have some (pot, coke, etc.)?

This is by no means a complete list of discussion points, but it can be a springboard from which you, parents and subject, can begin some meaningful dialogue. Notice that emphasis is always placed on putting the responsibility squarely back on the shoulders of the alcoholic.

Asking "What do *you* want to do about it?" and "Have you told your friends about treatment yet?" makes the onus light right where it should—with the young abuser.

If you haven't been told of the other substance abuse but are having some gut feelings about the matter, why not confront your child? You can say something like "Son, your mother and I have the strong feeling that you may be smoking dope. Can you help us with why we may be feeling that way?" Or "Honey, I'm having a gut-level feeling that you may be using some drugs. I know you haven't been drinking, but I'm having a real uneasy feeling. Can you help me with why I feel that way?"

These questions should be asked pretty much the way I have phrased them. They may seem awkward—not your style or in your own words—but they are worded specifically to prevent your son or daughter from going on the defensive and shifting the focus back to you!

Too often the temptation is to sit down immediately with your kid and ask that dangerous question, "Why?" Asking why just pushes the biggest defensive buttons that anyone has! For example:

PARENT: "Ted, *why* have you been up in your room smoking dope?"

TED: "My God! Now you're on my back accusing me of something else! Can't I do *anything* right around here?"

PARENT: "I never said you can't do anything right! I just asked you why you were smoking dope!"

TED: "You're getting paranoid about every time I'm up in my room! I feel like Big Brother's watching me!"

Well, that's enough to show you that you've lost control of the confrontation. Asking Ted why allowed him to turn the tables on you. He accused you of being paranoid and of being "Big Brother." He has shifted the focus to your behavior when the object was for you to confront him about *his* behavior!

This ability to shift the focus is a very real talent that alcoholics possess. They have been using it for as long as anyone has dared to confront them about their alcohol problem. The idea is simple: "If I [the alcoholic] can make you feel like you're the one who is to blame, then I will take the heat off me!"

By using the statements as I have phrased them, you are simply asking for a validation of *your* feelings. So, instead of asking why, you are asking the abuser for help with what's giving you certain gut-level feelings. You are providing him or her with an opportunity to explain *your* uneasiness, and in so doing, the abuser has the perfect opening to disclose the truth!

But suppose the young person counters with a straightforward denial about his or her substance use? That *is* a strong possibility, and there you are with the ball squarely back on your side of the net! If this happens, try these techniques:

"Well, I certainly *could* be wrong. But I need to reassure myself, and I hope you won't have any objection if I ask the treatment center to arrange for a drug screen (urinalysis), will you?"

Or: "Maybe I should just mention my suspicions to your counselor, and see what she thinks is causing me to be so suspicious of you!"

Either of these tools can be very effective. If other drugs are not being used, then there should be no reason to fear a drug screen test. You're telling your young person that it's to reassure you. The actual administration of such a test isn't as important at this stage of the game as the *idea* that the young abuser is going to be asked to take a drug screen test; at what exact hour or day is not disclosed. Therefore, if she is using other drugs, she runs the risk of being caught; she can't plan her drug use since she doesn't know when the test will be given.

By simply informing your young person that you are going to tell his counselor what you suspect, you may get the response you're after. Often, a patient is much more anxious to stay on the right side of the counselor or therapist because that person has greater power over him than the parent. Most of this power is centered in the fact that the therapist can terminate treatment if the patient fails to remain totally substance free.

But what *has* given you a feeling of uneasiness? What *has* led you to suspect that your son or daughter might have made a substance substitution? One of the biggest clues is a change in behavior. You should be on the lookout for changes in eating and sleeping habits. The young person who is so wound up that she just prowls the house all night long, working on this project or that, may be using cocaine or may be so pepped up on speed that the thought of sleep just isn't appealing.

The therapist or counselor you are working with will be

able to describe some other very specific kinds of behavior that might be even more indicative of other substance use.

For our purposes, I think your biggest clue lies in whether or not things seem to be going along *too easily.* Does that sound logical? Well, the treatment process is *not* easy. Learning to live without alcohol is a traumatic experience, and in the early stages enormous pressure is placed on the mind and the body of the individual attempting to recover.

The abuser may try to use another substance—Valium, let's say—to ease that pressure. When things seem to be going along smoothly, when it looks as if the treatment process is turning out to be a "piece of cake," I become concerned. So should you.

This is not to suggest that everyone going through treatment or attempting to stop drinking through AA finds it as difficult as I have said. We are dealing with individuals, and every case is specific to that individual. But on the whole, and considering that we are dealing with an *addictive* disease, giving up alcohol is tough! Therefore, when your young person tells you and perhaps others that he is "having no problems," it's time to think that another substance may be in the picture.

He or she may develop colds and flu symptoms and a whole host of other aches and pains that will necessitate a visit to the family doctor. You need to be very careful about the kinds of prescriptions that can come out of those visits. If your doctor is unaware that your son or daughter is working on an alcohol problem, the doctor might very well issue a sedative-type prescription, contrary to the best interests of the alcohol treatment.

This certainly doesn't mean that legitimate things won't crop up that definitely call for prescription medicine. It *does* mean that you should question the headache your daughter keeps getting that is so bad that she needs codeine-aspirin to treat it.

Prescription drugs can turn out to be the final substances

of choice if left unchecked, and you must not allow the trading of alcohol for a medicine chest full of new and other drugs!

So, as a general rule, it's a good idea to have an ear and eye tuned to how easy treatment and the removal of alcohol seem to be for the alcoholic. Remember, she can be a crafty, sly fox! She will sometimes try many different routes to avoid the ultimate confrontation about the problem. If your alcoholic thinks he is fooling you, if he is "doing all the right things," and still *it doesn't seem very hard*, I think you can allow yourself some suspicion about other substances being in the picture.

There are, of course, thousands and thousands of young alcoholics who simply have not had, and do not want any part of any other drug except alcohol. It would be a very unfair indictment to assume that every alcohol-abusing person also had an addiction to another substance! That's simply not the case. But there is enough dual addiction or dual usage among this age group to be concerned.

The ease with which the common "street drugs" such as marijuana, cocaine, and amphetamines are obtained makes this a fact of modern life. The kid who is not old enough to go into a liquor store or a bar, or who is unable to convince someone to buy for him, has no problem at all buying his dope right at school!

If you are one of those parents who still believe this is all fiction, you need to open your eyes and face the hard realities. Your young person can get almost any substance desired from sources too numerous to mention, quicker than you can fill your car's tank with gas!

Many school boards are considering adopting new locker-search procedures to combat the ever-growing pattern of students' bringing drugs and alcohol to school and keeping them there for continual daily and, many times, hourly use.

When you and your young person realize that something must be done about the alcoholism or alcohol abuse, it's a good time to question the possibility of dual substance abuse. Be open to discussion of this problem, as much as you have been open about alcoholism.

As a parent, you shouldn't assume that your young person has *not* been exposed to other substances. *All* young people today have been confronted with the decision to use or not use drugs.

Your open, approachable attitude will do wonders toward helping your son or daughter feel comfortable about confiding the whole story to you, if other drugs are being abused. *Lack of knowledge* of the problem will do more injury to you as parents than knowing the whole story.

Finally, be encouraged to get to the bottom of the total drug picture as painted by your young abuser. The treatment for use of marijuana, cocaine, amphetamines, Valium, and other sedative drugs will follow the same path as that for alcohol, and your treatment center will be prepared to deal with it.

Specialized treatment plans for, and places that deal with, abuse of other types of drugs, such as the opiates heroin, opium, and morphine, are available. Seek them out with the cooperation of your alcohol treatment program and keep attacking these problems as a family.

Stay on top of the situation by using the tools discussed in this book and be prepared to deal with other substance use with calm, rational thinking and affirmative action!

14

• • •

Did We Lose Us
in the Shuffle?

"I get the feeling you don't care about *me* anymore!"

"When are you going to spend a little time with *our* relationship?"

"Since this alcohol problem got started, our marriage has gotten worse!"

And it probably *has!* When a family begins the long road back to sobriety some things take their toll; one of them usually seems to be the relationship between you and your mate. This doesn't mean you necessarily will have marital difficulties. It only suggests that this is more often the case than not.

The reasons for this phenomenon are as diverse as the marriage relationships themselves. One thing appears to be evident; one theme appears over and over when a family member has the disease of alcoholism: guilt!

It often becomes necessary for one of the two spouses to affix blame for what has happened. It seems to make it easier if a husband or wife can point an accusing finger at the mate and say, "We wouldn't be in this mess if you had raised our child with more discipline!"

We refer to this as *throwing darts* because that's exactly what it turns out to be. You both arm yourselves with a bucket of verbal and psychological darts and then square off like two superpowers ready to press the "red button" and start a family holocaust! This is natural. It seems so logical to be able to trace the abusing person's alcohol problems to the way she was raised, to more tangible factors that we can reach out and touch, feel, experience.

There's no question in my mind that these are important factors, and we know that there are many psychological factors that enter into the alcohol abuse picture, factors that go hand in glove with the physical aspects of the disease.

The problem is that it becomes too easy to focus on these ancient facts of child-rearing as the cause of the problem the family is experiencing. That makes it even easier to affix the blame on one's mate. Example:

You are a working mother, and you've had to work for most if not all of your married life. You have managed to bear and rear your children, and you think that you have maintained a reasonably well-ordered home for all of you.

You have, by necessity, been away from home a lot. The day-to-day chores of traditional motherhood may have been passed around among several family members. You may have relied more on babysitters than you would have liked, but that's what your having to work demanded.

Nevertheless, it was nice to have the extra income; Christmases and family vacations were a little nicer because you were able to contribute your paycheck to the family coffers. Maybe you were even able to help your son or daughter buy a first car or start a college education with a sounder financial base than would have been possible if you had not worked. Then the alcohol problem rears its ugly head.

Now all the guilt for those years as a part-time homemaker come flooding out of the deep freeze where they have been harbored for who knows how many years. You start playing the "if" game, which goes something like this:

"If you didn't work," says hubby, "this never would have happened!"

"If I hadn't *had* to work, I could have stayed home!" (That's you throwing a dart back!)

"If you had been willing to move with me to L.A., you wouldn't have *had* to get a damn job!" (The darts are getting stronger!)

"Oh, yeah? If you had worked harder right here, you wouldn't have lost those promotions to other guys in the office and wouldn't have had to even *look* at taking a transfer!" (Not bad! She's learning what the really hurtful darts are!)

"Well, let me tell *you*, sweetie!" (Here comes his A-bomb dart!) If you didn't drink so damn much *yourself*, maybe I would have gotten more promotions! You *embarrass* me at every company party we've ever been to!"

Get the idea? Sure you do! The dialogue is mine, but you could have written your own "if" exchanges with your mate, and they probably wouldn't have been much different.

You both are feeling so guilty about the alcohol problem that it seems logical and necessary to put the *blame* for it squarely on someone else's shoulders. The fact that you both feel so much guilt over past behavior, even if that behavior was *justified and necessary*, urges you to open up the dart war and have at it!

If, indeed, there was a direct alcohol overuse or abuse by either one of you, it makes the throwing of those darts even more necessary, you think. When you start playing the "if" game and start the dart war, it's really hard for one of you to hoist the white flag of surrender! It sure does nothing for the relationship between the two of you except add further strain to an already overburdened set of nerves.

So, it's time to learn to use some new tools to help your relationship survive and even grow stronger through these difficult times.

1. You must learn to recognize when you are throwing a dart. You do this when you are aware that what you just said to your mate *feels too good!* This is a sign that you have been saving that statement up for a long time; you've just picked *now* to unleash it!
2. You must be willing to call time out. When the discussion is beginning to get out of hand, when you are feeling too angry to continue, you need to stop, at least for the moment.
3. One or the other of you has to focus the discussion on the *solution* to the problem, not on the cause.
4. You must be willing to deal with the grievances you have against each other, but not as a tie-in to the alcohol problem of your young adult.

These four new tools aren't as easy to learn as they may seem from a first read. Particularly vexing is the last one. You are aware that there is increased tension between the two of you because an alcohol problem has beset the family. This leads to some pretty hot discussions that probably get out of hand.

What you need to be able to do is call time out and say to each other, "This issue seems to be a biggie. But does it really have anything to do with Sandra's getting drunk?" Calling time out does not dismiss the problem; it only recognizes that tempers are getting out of hand, that the dart throwing is becoming too hot and heavy for you to handle, and that you need a break. It does not mean the issue is settled!

When either of you uses this time-out tool, it is naturally understood that the issue will come under discussion again, at some other time. You refocus on the alcohol issue. Say something like "Time out! I'm really angry about your bringing up *my* working! I agree that we need to talk about that, but right now we're discussing Sandy's problem!"

This won't be easy to do. You're in the heat of battle, and it's really hard to be the first one to run up the white flag. It might help to redefine the white flag. For you, the white flag doesn't mean total surrender. Rather, it means "time out." It means "We'll both agree to get back to this issue at another time, when tempers are more under control."

How do you do this? You write it down! Stop the discussion and immediately jot down on a "shopping list" the item to be brought up again. The best place to bring that item and other issues into play is with a therapist, a family or marital counselor, who will be part of the treatment you are undergoing as a family.

If you don't have such a person, find one! Go to your church or other place of worship; go to your local mental health center. Don't be shy; it's OK to have marital problems, but it's not OK to do nothing about them!

I use the term *shopping list* for these notations of issues because it's something you're used to dealing with. You've probably made hundreds of shopping lists in your married life, so why not make one more that will help you keep track of the issues that are at least as important as a loaf of bread or a carton of milk?

An important point in dealing with these four new tools for relationship-building is the point of nonescalation. It's too easy to let a discussion get out of hand and turn it into a real fighting match! That's called *escalating,* and it's something you both need to avoid. You do so by calling time out.

In *The Joy of Being Sober* (Contemporary Books, Inc., 1984) I suggest that couples actually form the letter *T* with their hands and say, "Time out!" It works! It will seem awkward to you at first, but the more you use this tool, the more it will become a recognized method of helping you both deal with critical but touchy issues, ones that are in danger of escalating into a full-blown war! If you can learn to stop escalating, you will accomplish a great deal in the process of communicating with less anger than before.

Attacking and blaming the other parent for the causes of the alcohol problem, then, must be laid to rest. You need to work on what it will take to defuse the questions that were posed in the beginning of this chapter, questions that obviously reflect hurt feelings and a sense of being abandoned by your spouse.

The questions also reflect something else: jealousy. A

great deal of your time and effort is going into the treatment process. You are spending hours that you certainly didn't believe you had before, going to meetings, therapy sessions, parents' groups, doctors' appointments, AA and Al-Anon meetings. In many cases, one parent tends to be more involved with the treatment than the other parent. The less involved parent isn't necessarily less concerned, but perhaps has less time to spend. The parent who is more involved often devotes all his or her time and energy to the alcoholic's treatment, and has very little of either left to share with his or her spouse by the day's end. Just as your other children may feel neglected while all the attention is paid to their sibling, so might the less involved spouse feel left out of the picture.

It makes a lot of sense, therefore, that your spouse is going to feel resentment, anger, and certainly *jealousy*, because all your efforts appear to be directed toward the son or daughter going through the recovery process. That's what makes reassessing your personal relationship with your mate so important.

You weathered measles, mumps, appendicitis, chicken pox, low or failing grades, car abuse, first dating, and myriad other ills and worries without falling apart, didn't you? Well, you can weather recovery from alcoholism or alcohol abuse, too. It's just that you tend to forget you are now dealing with another disease and that it has symptoms and get-well elements just like other diseases. What it *doesn't* have is a cure!

Now is the time for you and your mate to consider taking a personal break from the problems of alcoholism. Go away together for a weekend! One of the couples in our group decided to go on a Denver Bronco "road trip" right in the midst of one of the most difficult times in their son's alcohol and drug abuse treatment. This couple constantly used to worry, fret, and fight over the issues, blaming each other for the difficulties that were besetting them.

Their work in therapy and parents' group, along with their determination to get well again as a couple, gave them the strength to do this small thing for themselves.

152

"He's just going to have to be responsible for his own program of sobriety for this weekend," said the mother. "I've been wanting to see this game and we're going!"

"Will he take his Antabuse while you're gone?" asked another mother in the group.

"He damn well *better!*" she shot back. "But *that's his responsibility* from here on out. I'm not going to babysit him anymore! If Phil and I don't do something for ourselves, *we'll* be the ones in trouble!"

You can do similar things; maybe not an elaborate trip, but how about a weekend together at a local hotel? Isn't there some place in town, a new hotel or motel that looks appealing? Pack an overnighter and check in for a little "R and R." Find out if you're both still any good either at gin rummy or at romance! You'll be amazed at the results!

Just getting out of the house, trying a change of scenery, can improve your outlook. Your relationship has probably pushed itself to the breaking point as it is, what with additional expenses, perhaps for treatment, and even having one of your grown children back living at home!

Even if the alcoholic is one of your children who has not left home for the first time, you should consider getting away by yourselves. I recommend short two- or three-day vacations instead of long, involved trips. If you can do it, it's best for you both to take several of these short vacations during the course of alcoholism treatment.

Not only will you get much-needed rest and relaxation, but these jaunts are great for working on an item or two from your marital shopping list. Many items that have found their way onto the shopping list *while at home* might very well be dealt with and scratched off when a couple is in more serene, pleasant surroundings, with meals being served, dancing or in-room movies being enjoyed!

Suppose, for example, that "not spending enough leisure time together" is on your list. Well, while you are away together *doing just that* it becomes clearer that it wasn't quite that hard after all. What was needed was some kind of motivation to make necessary changes, to get off dead-center with your relationship as a couple and begin plan-

153

ning some time together. Again, let me stress that these brief vacations don't have to be elaborate. They can be a weekend spent hunting, fishing, backpacking, or just camping, if that's what you're into! Rolling up in *one* sleeping bag, inside a very private tent or camper, with no telephone or office messages to bug you, might be just the ticket.

One couple I know took off in the middle of their treatment program for their daughter and took up cross-country skiing. It was something they had always wanted to do, and when the pressures of their relationship were beginning to burst at the seams their therapist pushed this "action button," remembering they were both outdoorsy people.

It was the best thing they could have done! When they returned after four days in the Rockies they were new people. They had renewed their energies for life and for each other!

An important point about these vacations: Don't try to take other family members along, no matter how much pressure you may feel. Getting away with your mate takes priority over meeting some needs of the rest of the children, at least for the moment.

There will be other times when you can address the needs of your other children, as we will discuss in the next chapter. But for now, be selfish! Take some time for yourselves and let some of the tensions roll off your backs!

This is definitely a time for caring about each other. You are going through one of the most difficult periods of your parenthood, no matter how long you've been at that process or how many times you've done it.

The ability to keep staying power in the relationship is definitely put to the test. If one or the other of you comes to think that you're the guilty party for all that's happening, you might entertain the thought of just hitting the road, walking away from and out of the relationship.

If that's going to happen, then what will happen the *next* time there might be a relapse? Will one of you continue to threaten to leave again? If that gets started, it can be as dangerous as the most deadly dart in your arsenal.

If your alcoholic and the other kids in the family pick up on *that* message, you're going to have a whole different can of worms to deal with! More than once, an alcoholic young adult has overhead such a parental expression of threats, then promptly gotten roaring drunk just to speed the process of getting one parent or another out of the house (a parent he had had difficulty with all his life)! These can be very dangerous and perilous times for you as a couple, and you will constantly need to be on guard against such idle threats!

To say that sexual pressures are put on your relationship when an alcoholic youngster is occupying your attention is putting it mildly. The best of bed partners suddenly can turn to blocks of ice. Puzzlement and anger replace what used to be warm and passionate embraces, and the gap that is left in the marriage is felt keenly. Again, the guilt that is being shouldered by one or the other of you is the prime suspect!

Of course, your reasoning has told you, "It's my fault that Sandra is drinking too much. Maybe I'm spending too much time on Brenda [wife] and not enough time with Sandy!"

Does that make any sense? Can this tormented father replace his wife with his daughter? No! Certainly not sexually, but he begins to pay less and less attention to wife Brenda and more attention to daughter Sandra in a vain attempt to make up for what was lacking in her young life (lacking enough, perhaps, to cause her to drink too much).

And what locale does he pick for his refocused attention? Why, the bedroom, naturally! It's the one place that he has shared exclusively with his wife, but *now* we find Sandy being invited in with Daddy *and* Mommy, "just to pile up on the bed and watch some TV with us." Great Scot! Imagine what *that* does to Brenda's sex life!

But it happens and will continue to happen unless you are both attuned to the necessity of continuing to meet your own needs, even while going through the family recov-

ery process. Many women who have had few sexual problems will become temporarily dysfunctional when an alcoholic young person returns home to live. The question you
must answer for yourself is: Are you responding to the
problem of the alcoholic or to your own feelings of being
"inadequate" because you gave birth to an alcoholic?

Again on the distaff side, some women begin to withhold
the true measure of their sexual passions as a fitting method of punishing their mates for being the father of an
alcoholic! Doesn't seem fair, does it? It doesn't even make
much sense, but the human brain works in strange and mysterious ways, and sometimes the most remote of single
ideas tie themselves together to justify new, strange
behavior.

The sexual appetites of both partners need attention
during treatment and aftercare, perhaps more so than at
"normal" times. The vacations just discussed are real sexual rejuvenators—another reason I put them so high on the
list of solutions.

If the verbal dart throwing has been curtailed or stopped
altogether, then the bedroom and its related activities
sometimes become the new silent battleground for spouses
trying to deal with anger, guilt, shame, and denial about the
alcoholic.

You must guard against this, and one way is to keep the
lines of communication about sexual matters as open as
possible. Are you suddenly not feeling very stimulated
because a child is living in the house again? It might have
been several years since you've had to worry about anyone
else being in your house, and now you feel like your privacy
has been invaded. Call that for what it is and go on from
there! Isn't it possible that your young adult is going to go
out sometime? You might have to rearrange your love life
so as to take advantage of an empty house on Saturday
afternoons, say, but that's OK, isn't it?

Think of all the fun you two can have trying to find new
and different times and places to make love! I knew one
couple who decided to ditch all their kids on a Sunday and

drive their motorhome to a football game. They parked in their regular stadium spot, gave their seat tickets away, and proceeded to spend a long afternoon making love and watching the game on their portable TV! A variation on this occurred when the kids took their tickets and let Mom and Dad stay home! Same results, great idea!

So, to keep things sharp in your life, use the new tools that have been presented. Work hard at keeping the personal relationship between the two of you fresh, exciting, and as dynamic as possible under the circumstances. As in all of this treatment plan, don't be afraid to make changes—in the ways you think, act, and respond to the needs of your partner.

Practice creative listening; listen to what your mate is asking of you and to what you are feeling for him or her. Don't be afraid to express those special, loving feelings!

15
• • •
What about
My Other Kids?

"Does anyone care about *me?*"

"Sure! All you do *now* is bitch at *me* for *everything!*"

"Maybe *I* should get drunk! Then you'd start noticing me!"

Those are statements of real anger, of deep frustration, that are voiced many times by the brothers and sisters of a recovering alcoholic. Even though they may also be genetically predisposed to alcoholism, for one reason or another, they have not let alcohol become a problem.

But they definitely feel the impact of the alcohol problem in the family, and they don't know how to handle it. So many times these siblings become great enablers in their own right, trying desperately to adopt, or continuing, the role of the perfect kid.

The rationale is that if the sibling has the power to make everything right by being "perfect," then maybe the alcohol problem in the family will just go away and the family will be OK again.

These kids need special attention. They have been every bit as affected by the drinking as the abuser. Just think about the attention you have been paying to the alcoholic in the family. Perhaps that person has moved back into the family home, possibly displacing a younger brother or sister.

The additional fuss that parents will probably make over the returning "prodigal" son or daughter might be pretty strong stuff for the still-at-homes to handle. It's understandable, then, why they might try to overcompensate by acting out certain outrageous behaviors. They feel suddenly displaced by the person *and* the problem.

So now you have more than one problem to deal with: alcohol abuse *and* another kid (or maybe two or three!) who are all bent out of shape. Favoritism may have been a problem in your family from the very beginning. But now it is more important to recognize changing behavior and to confront it.

You can't afford just to let the other kids run all over you simply because you are preoccupied with the alcoholic. Yet that is what happens in many cases. Parents report that "just suddenly" little Stevie or Barbie has become a demon!

It didn't happen "just suddenly"; count on it! It has been smoldering and building for a long time, and the arrival back into the home of the alcoholic is just the excuse to let the garbage out of the bag!

If the alcoholic or alcohol-abusing young person has never left home, the same is true. Emphasis on the new problem is a good excuse to remind Mom and Dad that there are some other kids around the place who need attention. They often act in manners that are totally foreign to what you'd expect; they want and *need* your attention. They are also crying out for help and aren't sure what that help should be.

All they know is that *something's changed.* If your alcoholic has always been a "difficult" person, then maybe his siblings will accept this new condition as just one more example of brother or sister screwing up again!

159

However, the more the family, particularly the parents, become involved in the get-well process, the more the other kids in the family will require special attention. They will need to know several things, which you should tell them as soon as you are fully aware of them yourselves:

1. The alcohol abuse is a problem for *everyone,* not just the person suffering with the disease at the moment.
2. It is entirely possible the same thing could happen to them!
3. They are part of the problem and must be part of the solution, too. That means they must be willing to participate in the various group therapies that will be suggested as a course of treatment.
4. You have not stopped loving them!
5. Outrageous behavior on their part is not the way to get your attention and will not be tolerated!
6. They must not try to "rescue" the alcoholic anymore.

This last point really hinges on understanding the enabling process. Just as you, the parents, have been enabling your alcoholic not to face the consequences of his or her alcoholic behavior, so do other brothers and sisters.

They rush to the "rescue," to make things easier and generally to cover up many of the alcoholic's behaviors in order to try to keep the family boat on an even keel.

Much as you did, they believe they are *helping,* when in fact they are just enabling the alcoholic to avoid facing his or her problem. So, you must begin a program with those other siblings to get them to understand the differences between helping and enabling.

It is quite OK to offer to go to the store for the alcoholic brother 'or sister if circumstances *other than drinking* prevent him or her from going. That's being helpful. Going to the store for the alcoholic who's simply hung over or still drinking and doesn't want to go is gross enabling!

That's a very simple example. Other kinds of sibling behavior in the enabling category include:

1. loaning money
2. making or changing appointments for the alcoholic

3. loaning vehicles
4. not reporting relapses or "tiny slips"
5. lining up jobs

All family members participate in many other enabling actions, making it easy for the alcoholic one to do very little to help himself! These are just a few that are most common among the other children in a family.

It's particularly hard for a sibling to refuse the loan of a car or cash. The promises to make it "just one more time," or to "pay it back as soon as I get my new job" can be pretty tempting. If the alcoholic throws in some sort of reward, then the pressure is really on. Rewards such as "I'll pay you back with seven percent (or whatever) interest" sounds pretty good on the surface.

But everyone needs to remember that we are dealing with the crafty mind of the alcoholic, and most times the loans will go the way they always have: down the tubes! I think it's a good idea just to establish ground rules from the beginning:

"George, let's have an understanding. I'll help you anyway I can, but don't ask me for money! Mom and Dad can deal with that end of things with you; please leave me out!"

Whatever bad feelings may have been brought to the surface by this statement can be dealt with *right then* and not left for another time (say, when the loaned money is due and can't be repaid). How does the sibling handle those bad feelings? He or she says, "I love you, George, and I care about you. If I loan you money, I'm just helping you avoid the understanding of what you need to do for yourself!"

There's not much point in asking the sibling to point out that George wouldn't need to borrow money if he hadn't been drinking his own paycheck or allowance; George will get enough of that reinforcement from others, including the parents. It's enough for the sibling to strengthen the bonds of love and caring and reinforce the fact that it is *because* of this loving and caring that the loan is being refused.

Handing out sums of money simply delays George's get-well process and doesn't do anything for the sibling's get-well program either.

The other taboo is loaning a car to the recovering person. There are exceptions, just as there would be times when *you* would loan your wheels to your child. The exceptions are:

1. when a car is needed to keep a treatment program date
2. when a car is needed for a doctor's or dentist's appointment
3. when the recovering person is going to an AA meeting
4. when *agreed-upon chores* are being shared and a car is necessary to complete those chores

I consider loaning of money and cars the most important of the enabling practices in which brothers and sisters of the alcoholic become trapped. Once these practices begin, it's very hard to back out of them, and then more guilt is felt by the siblings—guilt born of having to say "no."

Siblings certainly try to "make up for" this family problem of alcohol abuse in other ways. The alcoholic's sibling might suddenly start to cry, shout, use foul and abusive language, and so on. This kind of behavior has to be confronted with care, love, and concern, no matter how badly you may want to kick the little darlings in the butt and do your own kind of shaping-up program! Use the phrase *I wonder* to try to get at the root of the problem:

"I wonder, Sue, if you can tell me what you think is making you act like this."

"I wonder, Brian, if this is what you're *really* feeling."

You get the idea. You may feel like you're playing the idiot, but it works! It is a tool designed to help your other children take a reflective look at how they may be coming across to others. It also gives them a chance to correct the behavior by answering your "I wonder" questions with a new or changed statement.

Another tool for use with this inappropriate behavior is to be more directly confrontational with a question such as

"Trish, what is it *I'm* doing that makes you say that to me?" Or try this one: "Sounds like you're really angry with me, Trish. Is that what I'm hearing?"

These bits of dialogue might sound very awkward to you at first, but once you have mastered the techniques, you will be amazed at the results.

All of these tools are designed to help you get your other children to admit *their feelings,* instead of just responding to your feelings or those of the recovering person in the family.

You may want to explore the many ways you can get closer to your other children during this period, when the family is in crisis over the alcoholism issue. How long has it been since you went to the zoo together? to a family picnic? to a movie? In other words, you can use this crisis to reestablish some of the togetherness that families let slide all too often.

Too much giving on your part can also be easily misunderstood, and it will be necessary for you to treat your other children in as normal a fashion as possible. They must not think that they are being rewarded just because the alcohol problem is not theirs. Rather, reaffirm your love for *all* your children, whether they have a difficult problem or not.

Let's wrap up this whole sibling business by looking at the story of Holly and Heather, two sisters living in the same household. Heather, nineteen years old, was the recovering alcoholic. She had had a difficult time in college and had dropped out during the first semester of her sophomore year, a victim of too much partying and not enough concentration on studying.

When it was diagnosed that Heather was indeed abusing alcohol, that she was alcoholic in both her psychological and her physical behaviors, she came back home to live and entered treatment.

Her twelve-year-old sister, Holly, was an average student and was enjoying the same kind of popularity with her school chums that Heather had become famous for. The girls had a ten-year-old brother, Jeffrey, who pretty much just "did his own ten-year-old-thing," as the parents phrased it.

Heather had used up most of her college loan funds and was "on the dole" from her parents for every dime. She was not well enough to hold a job, nor did she have any particular skills other than waiting on tables, which didn't seem to interest her.

The parents worked out a contract with Heather that would allow her to assume several major chores in the family household, for which the father, Greg, was willing to pay. This, the parents reasoned, was a fair trade; they needed things done at home, and Heather needed a way to make at least a few dollars a day to provide for some of her personal needs.

Holly had been delighted to have Heather back home. She had missed her big sister, in spite of the age difference between them. She had assumed Heather's room as an additional room for her own slumber party guests and had made some minor changes in the room to suit her own needs. But when Heather came home Holly quietly and quickly rearranged everything just the way it had been.

Greg and wife Marj had explained Heather's alcohol problem to both Holly and Jeffrey. The plan was for both of the siblings to enter the family portion of the treatment program at the appropriate point in the schedule.

Among the chores assigned to Heather on a regular paid-for basis was preparation of the evening meal. This was to free Marj, who had been holding down a responsible, difficult full-time position that often kept her at her office later than Greg. It was an ideal thing for her to be able to come home to a meal already prepared, and she was delighted with the way Heather took over with great gusto for the first few weeks.

However, Holly quickly began to be manipulated by her older sister. Holly's school schedule brought her home from school quite early in the afternoon, after starting classes very early in the morning. At first Heather complained of seeming to be "under the weather" and "depressed." She cautioned Holly not to "say anything to Mom and Dad for fear they would just worry." Instead, Heather suggested Holly might help her out with the dinner preparations just "until I get to feeling better." Holly was delighted to cooperate—at first. She had always been responsible for clearing the dinner table. Her brother Jeffrey emptied trash and loaded the dishwasher as part of his regular household contributions.

Holly now began to do more and more of the cooking, saying nothing about Heather's "blues," as she called them. Heather began to lie on the couch or, more often than not, just go to her room to lie down. Holly kept her mouth shut, eager to be doing something to please her older sister.

Secretly, Holly was feeling like an important part of Heather's get-well process. After all, Heather was suffering from a disease, and whatever anyone could do to help her shouldn't be begrudged!

But the more Holly did for Heather (enabling), the more Heather demanded. Holly began to assume other chores assigned to Heather, chores for which Heather was being paid! When Marj and Greg complimented Heather on a particular meal, Heather would graciously include Holly in the praise by saying something like "Holly really helped me a lot!"

Holly took over the packing of lunches for everyone, something else that Heather was assigned. When brother Jeffrey noticed how many times it was Holly, not Heather, preparing his lunch, his mother's sack lunch, *and* her own, he was ready to bail Holly out.

"Does Mom know you are doing Heather's stuff?" he asked.

Holly admonished him not to say anything for fear of upsetting Heather and throwing her back into drinking. They had all heard of the possibility of relapse, and Holly certainly didn't want the responsibility for that! Heather would reenter the chores picture just enough to prevent it from looking like she had abandoned the whole project, and Jeffrey would forget about the many times he saw Holly doing Heather's assigned and paid-for work.

Heather had severe menstrual cramps, and "her days" would put her to bed for most of the time. Holly also suffered discomfort during her period, but *she* suffered in silence. As bad as it was for her, Holly continued to pick up more and more of the slack left by Heather—during good days and bad. It made no difference to Holly.

And then the inevitable happened. Holly, arriving home much earlier than usual because of a scheduled teachers' planning conference, caught Heather with a beer in her hand, being very chipper indeed on a day in the middle of her "bad days."

Holly was furious! All the deep-seated anger sprang to the surface in a flurry of fists and expletives that made Heather cringe. It was one thing for Holly to help Heather secretly by doing her work for her, but when Heather returned to drinking it was the final straw! A very angry Holly blurted out the whole story to her parents, who were shocked and dismayed.

"But why didn't you tell us?" Marj inquired.

"I didn't want Heather to *have* to go back to drinking because there was too much work!" shouted Holly. "But she *cheated* on me!" she fairly screamed.

Jeffrey was terribly confused by the whole turn of events. *He* had assumed that both he and Holly felt a deep sense of responsibility for Heather's sobriety. He had kept quiet for the same reason—not wanting to upset Heather and thus cause the relapse.

Heather was required to renew some terms of her contract with her parents, and it was determined that Holly would see a therapist at the treatment center on an individual basis for a short while to help her deal with the sudden flow of anger at her sister.

Both Greg and Marj made a concerted effort to step up their personal interest in their two younger children, while making it abundantly clear that Heather was solely responsible for her own sobriety. In therapy sessions it was

166

revealed that Heather had been drinking secretly for some time since she began to realize she could count on her sister to enable her to continue life pretty much as it had been.

Was Heather a "bad" alcoholic, a "bad, scheming bitch" (as Marj shouted in a session)? No, indeed. Heather was just an *alcoholic*, playing the same kinds of games alcoholics have played and continue to play. To her, whatever it took to try to fool everyone about her sobriety was what she was going to do. The fact that she had a cooperating sister and, in some respects, a cooperating brother was just another plus.

Holly and Jeffrey, but particularly Holly, had to reexamine their feelings about Heather and how she "could do this to me." With therapy, Holly was able to disgorge her rather large bag of garbage about her family situation. When she and Jeffrey entered their respective therapy groups they had a fine opportunity to begin to learn to deal with their feelings.

Holly and Heather rebuilt a relationship, a new one that took into consideration the fact that they were both dealing with Heather's disease, but in different ways—Heather by temporarily dropping the tools of recovery and Holly by allowing herself to be a pawn in that game because she was afraid to be the cause of Heather's return to drinking!

Heather made a new commitment to treatment, and Holly stopped being the "little mother" who was enabling everyone in the family. Greg and Marj, realizing the neglect they had allowed to creep into their relationship with their younger children, made renewed efforts to treat Holly and Jeffrey with new respect and a great deal of individual attention.

Heather and the disease of alcoholism were no longer the main topic of conversation among them, as it had been in the past. Jeffrey and his dad began to do things together again. Holly and Marj began to go "mall crawling" without having Heather tag along. Generally speaking, the family began to place the responsibility for Heather's sobriety where it had always belonged—with Heather!

The assumption of chores may seem like no big deal. But to a sensitive twelve-year-old girl who idolized her older sister, it was a way she could further advance in the esteem of her big sis and also make what Holly thought was a significant contribution to her sister's recovery from alcoholism! It all seems so logical, doesn't it?

So the siblings of an alcoholic require a special kind of understanding. It doesn't really matter if they are younger or older than the recovering person. What's important is the manner in which you respond to their needs, the manner in which you attune yourselves to recognizing those needs and meeting them, and knowing when to do so is beneficial and not detrimental.

Nobody said recovery was easy! But it has many rewards, such as the closeness family members can experience when they come through difficult times together. No one will ever, for example, take Holly for granted again!

Don't be afraid to sit down with your other children. Talk to them! Listen to them! Respond to them as individuals who need your love, affection, attention, and discipline as much as the recovering young adult in your family.

The rewards for parents in following this plan are enormous! Why, you might even remember that you really do *have* other children, and they can be an inspiration to the entire family with their energies, emotions, and willingness to get into the fight against alcoholism and alcohol abuse, just like you!

16

• • •

It's Dark
When You Walk
in the Shadows

"Mirror, mirror on the wall, am I as pretty as my mom?"

"I tried to think about law school, but Dad's such a hotshot legal beagle, I knew I couldn't cut it!"

"God! I'm so tired of Mom wanting to be my friend! Couldn't she just be my *mother?*"

This is competition of a different sort—not the kind that's expected between outstanding young athletes or scholars, but the razor-sharp competition between parent and child. Does it sound out of the realm of possibility for you? Think about it!

There are so many times when compliments are paid to you within earshot of your children. How many times have you had people remark on your looks or your latest business triumph? Are you constantly receiving accolades for your tennis, golf or running program?

There certainly isn't anything wrong about being blessed with beauty, talent, skills, aptitudes of all kinds. It's the ideal way of life, isn't it? We want the very best for our children, and we certainly don't see anything wrong if we continue to keep *ourselves* in the best of mental and physical shape! But when you are dealing with an alcoholic or alcohol-abusing youngster you are dealing with a fragile ego. No matter how handsome he is, no matter how smart she is, the son or daughter in trouble with alcohol will invariably admit to believing he or she just doesn't quite measure up to the parents' expectations.

Many times we have witnessed family conjoint sessions in which a beautiful young woman confesses in front of her mother that she just "never will be as pretty as you, Mom!" So what does this young woman do? She *drinks* to compensate. She begins to abuse alcohol as a means of making herself totally different from her beautiful mother.

The real tragedy occurs when the mother hears such a statement from her daughter. Mom, in most cases, has had no idea that she was a direct source of competition for her daughter! It's almost inconceivable to most women to think that they are competing with their daughters, yet in the instances of alcohol abuse this pattern becomes all too often evident.

The young man who was debating entering law school really did have the desire and the capability to do well in law school. The thing that was holding him back was the *fear* that he would not do as well in the profession as his illustrious father! He never tried, but instead turned more and more to the use of alcohol as a means of compensating for the gap he felt existed between his father and himself!

Does this mean that Mother and Dad should hold back? Of course not. Nor does it mean that sons and daughters should not have parental examples of achievement to help guide their own lives. It simply means that perhaps you, the parents, have not *realized* the intense, underlying competition that has been formed in the mind of your young alcoholic.

The same competitive edge can be found among siblings, with similar results. A family in treatment recounted the tale of many family get-togethers. The "successful" brothers, sisters, and assorted sons-in-law and daughters-in-law all seemed to have so much more than the alcoholic son. The alcoholic young man and his pretty young wife had every bit as much talent, beauty, and ability as the other children of the successful parents. Yet this young couple sulked at family reunions, feeling as if they weren't quite "good enough." Neither had completed college or established a permanent career. Alcohol, and numerous relapses, had just helped reinforce the idea that somehow they were "different."

Try as they might, the parents fought a never-ending battle against this unseen but strongly felt adversary in the family. Even the other siblings had a deep sense that the alcoholic son was being "too hard" on himself, and was not "realizing his hidden potential."

That's well and good! But try to tell that to the only one of four children who has been struck by the disease of alcoholism! He just adds the disease to his long list of personal failures, denigrating himself for not being quite up to par with the rest of the family! Many times his father and mother would share with our parents' group the frustration they were experiencing at trying to help their son and his wife overcome this feeling. But the fact remained that only this son had been inflicted with the alcoholism, at least at that time.

It became necessary to encourage the alcoholic and his wife to set personal goals that were different from any other family member's; to get them to understand that they were unique individuals and, as such, could afford to build their lives in distinct and separate manners. They would not have to live up to impossible models set by the other sisters and brothers.

In another case, a mother turned out to be the best jump-roper among her daughter's friends. When the current physical fitness craze was well established, this mother's college-age daughter proudly brought some of her roommates home for a short school break.

Packed among their possessions were the girls' exercise

171

jump ropes. At the first appearance of this equipment Mother showed up in her leotard and tights, fresh from her own exercise class. She promptly gave the girls an exhibition of real jump rope skill!

Mother was a natural athlete. She had been an outstanding phys. ed. major in college and had pursued a degree in physical education and coaching. Marriage cut short her career goal, and she never got the coaching job she sought, but she *did* teach phys. ed. for two years after college.

Her daughter, a talented and bright girl in her own right, was just not the natural athlete that her mother was, and the jump rope incident turned out to be a further demonstration of her own perceived inadequacy.

Mom, of course, had no idea that she was her daughter's own most severe competitor. They had grown up together—Mom and kid were "pals" and "bosom buddies." The problem was that daughter Alicia had severe alcohol abuse problems.

Seeing Mom out there skipping rope like the pro she was simply added to Alicia's already low self-esteem. She got roaring drunk that night, much to the embarrassment of her parents, her school friends, and herself. The competition between mother and daughter was, of course, one-sided.

The mother, Monique, had absolutely no idea that her daughter considered her such a threat. In conjoint sessions between mother and daughter, instance after instance of this feeling surfaced. The boyfriends that Alicia had brought to her home always made remarks to Alicia about how beautiful Monique was; that her mother had a dynamite figure; that it must be fantastic to have a mother who was so beautiful.

To Alicia it wasn't fantastic at all! It was hell! It was a private, gnawing kind of hell that only continued to help her feed her alcohol problem. Long-term therapy was one of the things that helped Alicia learn to cope with this problem and with the new relationship that emerged between mother and daughter.

Over and over again, parental pressures are applied in this competitive arena, generally without the parents' conscious knowledge that they exist. It's only when the alcohol problem emerges as a point of reference that *all* aspects of a family's interpersonal dealings come into the examination room. This is another strong point for the generally accepted practice of insisting that the family enter treatment along with the recovering person.

So now we get to the nagging question, "Have I spent too much of my time being a buddy to my kid(s), instead of being a parent?" Honestly, you may have. In the cases of young alcoholic adults and their parents with whom I have worked I have found an almost universal thread: One or both parents were using their offspring to help *meet their own unfulfilled needs.*

"My son is going to have the college education that I never had" is a frequently heard statement along these lines. Another example: "There's no reason why my daughter can't marry rich; it's just as easy as it is to marry poor! And she certainly has the looks for it!" The "buddy" act comes into play when Mom and/or Dad begin to do things with the kids to help meet their own unfulfilled goals. Thus, the father spends hours helping his kid with complicated homework, pushing him perhaps beyond his natural capabilities, hoping for a college scholarship. Even more prevalent is the father who, day after day, hour after hour, goes out to "throw the ball around" with his son who has big-time athletic promise.

The mother who belonged to a college sorority may automatically think this is the best thing for her daughter, too. But is it? How much pressure can be applied to an already fragmented ego that is searching for itself and turning more and more to alcohol for temporary answers?

Yet under the buddy system you will find mothers acting more like sorority sisters to their daughters than like mothers. Everything that is done during high school may be geared with an eye to making sure the daughter gets a bid from several college sororities.

If the daughter is assured of a "legacy bid" (an invitation tendered with special consideration paid to mother's membership) then buddy pressure can even be intensified. It becomes important, says Mom, that her daughter learn to get the best wardrobe for the money, date only boys who seem to be fraternity or at least college material themselves, etc. I have known mothers who have literally helped their precollege daughters shop for both clothes *and* men!

Remember the nature of the disease that is alcoholism. It builds a psychological dependency along with a physical one, allowing many elements of childhood experiences to be brought into play to help nurture the disease.

The lack of parental discipline where it is so clearly called for simply feeds the enabling process. So many times a young alcoholic shares with his therapist the knowledge that he could "always get away with it."

Confronted with these enabling patterns, the parents repeatedly deny there was a lack of discipline, claiming instead, "Charles never gave us any trouble whatsoever!"

For the young alcoholic this sets a firm pattern: *Nobody* is going to say anything derogatory about her alcoholic behavior; *nobody* is going to do much confronting, *even though the alcoholic may be demanding it!* Why? No one said anything because, in all probability, the discipline void was created a long time ago, and the alcoholic behavior was being treated as something that "he'll outgrow!"

"I raised hell myself when *I* was in college," the father sitting in the therapy room proudly proclaims. "But *I* knew when to stop!" Well, good for him! Unfortunately, he has an alcoholic son who *doesn't* and *can't* stop drinking! Dad ignored early warning signs and failed to practice discipline that would have given him a little more knowledge of his son's behavior patterns and, most of all, have made him unafraid to confront those behaviors.

This certainly is not meant to be misconstrued as saying you "pound alcoholism or alcohol abuse out of your kid!" Quite the contrary. What is meant is that you should make changes in the ways you treat the alcoholic young person in

174

your life. You go back to being a parent; thus the reason for the contract we discussed in earlier chapters.

What you have done in the past cannot be continued, or the chances are very real that what you are now going through will be repeated. It is essential that the young alcoholic understand that, no matter the age difference, parental authority must be reestablished.

Certain things will, of course, be different. You can't very well discipline a twenty-year-old to make him keep his room clean in the same way as you would a ten-year-old. However, the twenty-year-old *can* have a very clear understanding that a messy room in an otherwise clean family home will *not* be considered acceptable behavior!

We have already covered much of this ground in the chapters dealing with contracts and enabling behavior. But as a parent, you must understand, as part of your own recovery, that withholding discipline has been a contributing factor to your child's problem.

Your child believes he can do nothing that will get him into serious trouble with you, so he keeps treating life and *its* disciplines and responsibilities in the same fashion. The problem with that, of course, is that the rest of the world in which he must function for the rest of his life may not be willing to overlook such behavior.

The young person who is constantly tardy for work or for classes must eventually pay the penalty! How long can the dean, the job supervisor, the new husband or wife put up with childish, undisciplined behavior from a supposedly grown-up individual? Not very long! There will be penalties for such behavior, and the young person will receive an all-too-rude awakening to the way things really are out there!

You must not castigate yourself; what is done is done. Remember when we mentioned that the life script is written for most people at age four or five? You can't undo what has already been done, but you *can* change the way things are going to be done in the future.

It's not as hard to give up being a buddy as it may seem. You can learn to be a *friend*, someone who is easily accessible, perhaps for the first time in your relationship with your son or daughter. Think about it! How many times have you really been available just to sit and listen to what your offspring is saying to you? I often find myself lacking in this area and am always open to being reminded by my four young-adult children that I *must listen* to what they are saying!

You exchange buddyism for friendship when you stop trying to do things with your children as an equal, a peer. Instead, you revert to the role of parent and friend. Here's a simple example:

A father was playing racquetball with his daughter, who was in treatment for alcohol abuse. The father consistently handed defeat after defeat to his daughter, whipping her soundly on the courts. It had not occurred to him that maybe he should be playing more with men his own age who were better matched to his own athletic prowess. He wanted to spend time with his daughter and felt that he was his "daughter's best friend" and therefore was "happy to be giving so much time" to her.

But his daughter was telling her therapist that she wished "Dad would play with Mom, or someone else, and let me play with my own friends more!"

"What makes you unwilling or unable to tell your father this?" asked the therapist.

"God! I don't want to *hurt* Dad!" she fairly cried. "He seems to *enjoy* our games so much!"

When father and daughter came into conjoint therapy, they were able to talk about their buddyism. Now they have a new set of rules. If racquetball is the plan, then the father will arrange to play perhaps two games with his daughter before turning the court over for the rest of the time to one of his daughter's friends.

Father has even rescheduled his own playing time with his own peers, including his wife, so that he will not always be at the court at the same time as his daughter. He is learning to emancipate two people in this relationship: himself and his daughter.

What the father has learned is that he was looking at his daughter and the resulting buddyism as a substitute for his own loneliness! It had been a long time since he had approached his wife, asking her to take time from a busy schedule to meet him at their athletic club for a game or two.

When the wife/mother was confronted with this, it came as no surprise to the therapist that her answer was, "I didn't think Paul wanted me to *interfere* with what he and Peg were doing together! They always have so much *fun* together!"

It was a complete surprise to all the family members that they had let such a thing happen to them. The roles had become terribly confused between father and daughter and between husband and wife. It took very little time for them to restructure what their proper perspectives should be, and they began to make other improvements in their family relationship as well.

Daughter Peg no longer could use Dad's superior playing ability as an excuse to "have a little drink just to loosen up"; she had to face squarely the fact that she had been using her father in a competitive arena for much of her young adult life and that Dad was, indeed, the competition she most feared.

So, begin to look at your relationships in the light of what we have been talking about in this chapter. Ask yourself these questions:

1. Am I the main competition?
2. If I *am*, in what areas? How can I stop?
3. Have I been trying to meet my needs through my kids? How? What can I do to stop?
4. Have I been more buddy than parent? How?

Work on these! Go ahead and put discipline back to work as an important tool of love. Most importantly, learn to feel OK as a noncompetitive parent. It's easier!

17

. . .

Have You Hugged Your Kid Today?

This is a chapter about nurturing, that rather nebulous process between human beings from the moment of birth through death. Anyone who has held a small child in his arms and found himself cuddling and cooing and going through all kinds of facial contortions knows what *nurturing* means!

When we apply nurturing to the young adult or teen-aged alcoholic we can find some rather interesting pieces that fit into a complicated jigsaw puzzle. So often in treatment it comes to the surface that an abusing young person "never felt loved" by one or both parents. This always comes as a mammoth shock to most parents, who feel they have done just the opposite: They have *lavished* their offspring with love!

Yet, on further probing in therapy, the little, seemingly insignificant things begin to rise to the surface like tiny bubbles. There is the mother who worked during most of the growing-up stages of her kids' lives; there's the father who traveled almost constantly, particularly during the important formative years.

When Mom came home from work there was no question that her attention would be focused on her children for the hours that they were awake in the evening. But most of the *nurturing* may have been provided by a daycare center, a babysitter, or older brothers or sisters who were responsible for "watching things" until a parent arrived home. And when Dad returned from his many trips he came bearing many gifts, laden like one of the Oriental kings! Everyone would crowd around him to receive the little remembrances from this city or that, but the *nurturing* Dad would have provided by being around was lost.

Does this mean that mothers should not work just because they have children? Of course not. That's absurd and totally impractical considering the lifestyles that we Americans have enjoyed for so many years. Neither should Dad give up his lucrative and important position with his company because there is travel involved.

Besides, at this stage of the game, whatever has happened has happened! You can't go back and "pull" Dad off the road; you can't jerk Sonny out of daycare and have Mom quit her job! That's all behind you now that the kids are grown. So what *can* you do?

You can begin to understand what nurturing meant to the alcoholic and why changes in the ways that families deal with the problem are so important to secure recovery. I certainly am not suggesting that all the alcoholic's problems can be traced and firmly linked to the parents' manner of rearing children.

It is a fact, however, that the bottle becomes the main source of nurturing for the alcoholic. You see, the bottle never travels, never has to leave the home to earn a living, never has to do anything but provide solace and comfort!

The alcoholic can always count on the bottle. It's always *there*. Does that sound odd or improbable? If you stop and think that the chemical your young adult is consuming is a powerful one—one that works the same way every time—

you will begin to understand how alcohol can become the principal nurturing element in your son's or daughter's life.

Is she depressed? Take a drink! Is he not handsome enough? Take a drink! Has promotion passed her up again? Take a drink! And the alcohol does its temporary job. One time a client told his therapy group that he was glad for his sobriety because "now I don't have to spend a lot of time and money *drinking those girls 'pretty'!"*

Everyone laughed, of course, but the sad fact is that he was right. His nightly forays into the popular "fern bars" found him sitting at the bar drinking and buying drinks for any girl he thought he had a chance to score with. He was not making any attempt at matching like interests, backgrounds, and so on.

The alcohol that he consumed made him feel like they were all "dynamite ladies" (his words), and it was only after sobering up that he would realize that he had once again made severe errors in judgment about his female companions. The same, of course, applied to the ladies.

Because the singles bars are the mecca for this age group, alcohol is the natural nurturing element. The plain girl feels prettier; the short, balding male feels worthy of competition; the couple with absolutely nothing in common allow alcohol to comfort them into thinking they were ideal for each other.

So what do you, as parents, do now? Is it really too late for you to go back to some of the basics of hugging, holding, kissing, and embracing that you engaged in when your youngsters were small? No it isn't too late, but it may be very awkward!

How many times have you said, either aloud or just in your mind, "I just wasn't brought up to hug and kiss!" or "My father *never* had me sit on his lap!"

We are products of our own scripting. If those things didn't happen to *us*, how in the world are we ever going to pass them along to our own children? It's a sad thing to see a mother who has been separated from her daughter for a number of months greet that child at the airport with not much more than a perfunctory grasp of the hand.

My therapist friend Ty Owens would *never* let me or anyone else get away with that! If you are within ten feet of Ty in a hallway or any public place, you can count on a warm bear hug from this kind and tender giant!

Often at airports I make it a point to observe families greeting each other. How sad that so-called social convention or old family taboos make it seemingly impossible for fathers to hug their sons, to say, "I love you!" and to take an extra moment for a truly genuine embrace!

My son and I went through a period of time, during my own severe and active alcoholism, when I let that drop. There wasn't a whole lot about me to love, I'm sure, and it has taken the process of recovering for us to reestablish what was always there but submerged in a sea of alcohol.

Now, when we greet each other from opposite ends of the country, when my travels bring me to New York, we don't care who sees two grown men embracing and making a genuine display of love and warmth. It's called nurturing! And as a parent, *I* need it as much as my children!

That's the message you need to understand. It doesn't really matter what you did before the alcoholism; what matters is *now* and the commitment you are willing to make to change. Show me a mother and daughter who are bashful about exchanging kisses, and I'll show you a wife who complains of being "abused" in her bedroom by a husband who is "too demanding!"

These qualities of closeness—the feeling of one human being for another—become an important replacement for that nurturing bottle. Remember that, when alcoholics give up the bottle, they are giving up their best friend!

Does that bother you? Are you feeling threatened by the idea that a chemical could be considered a best friend? Don't be; it's true. As we have said so many times before, the bottle never lets you down if you are an alcoholic. And for most young people who have become alcoholic, who have developed both a psychological and physiological dependence on the drug, *life* has let them down!

181

As parents it's so difficult to believe that the *only* times your young people feel even adequate is when they are drinking! You look at the potential of your children, all the historical family background of success, and say, "Hogwash! My son is carrying on the family traditions! He is going to be successful just like me, and my father and *his* father. . . ."

Of course no one looked at the same family trait of predisposition to alcoholism until it finally struck with awesome force in *your* son or daughter!

So, you begin all over again by tossing out what was in the past. I call this *idea resuscitation.* As in the procedure for reviving a drowning victim, parents must say to themselves, "Out with the old ideas; in with the new!"

The old ideas were based on old traditions, on conforming to what social mores in your family seemed to dictate. I once treated a woman who hid behind her Norwegian background as the reason for her "cold attitudes" toward her husband and her children! Well, it made sense to her because that was how *she* had been brought up by *her* parents. They never, she said in her therapy sessions, exchanged kisses with one another, even at bedtime. When the hour came for the children to retire they *shook hands* with father and kissed mother ever so lightly on a turned cheek!

The same woman could not understand why her own children felt so estranged. They were of a different generation, a generation that showed them that open displays of affection were OK, and they wanted some of that demonstrative affection from their mother! She was incapable of giving it; to her, embracing and kissing, particularly in public, were totally unacceptable.

When the same woman took her beautiful blond daughter out of the de-tox center of a local hospital, she simply could not bring herself to embrace the young woman, just to *hold* her. It was too foreign to the mother's own life script, even though her daughter literally begged for the comfort of her mother's arms!

When the daughter continued to have periodic relapses and both mother and father had to bail her out of one situation after another, they began to realize that something was definitely missing in their daughter's life. Their daughter's choice of boyfriends appalled the parents. They seemed so "unsavory, coarse, and common." Daughter would rebel, saying, "But he *loves me!* He gives me what I want and *need!*"

The parents thought *they* had provided their blond "goddess" with everything anyone could imagine wanting. She had the best of clothes, a sports car, a college education. When it was time for a coming-out party the girl was given one of the finest at a leading hotel.

The girl had everything, all right, except the *nurturing* that she desperately sought, and this she found in the bottle and in "unsavory" (*unconventional* would have been more accurate) male friends. In family therapy it became very evident that the daughter wanted to share some warmth with her parents. The material things had been wonderful, but they certainly had not met the needs of this alcoholic personality.

It took a long time for that family to get used to the idea of being open with their feelings; a lot of old tapes had to be replaced with new ones—ones that said, "It's really OK to show you I love you!"

This certainly is not an isolated example; it happens over and over, and you need only change the reasons from "ethnic background" or "the way I was brought up" to any number of other excuses to find where nurturing has been a missing vital ingredient.

Parents become stuck with the same problems over and over. They must not allow themselves to go on another guilt trip! It's so easy to wail and moan, "We've *obviously* not done *anything* right," that parents mire themselves in a mud hole so deep it becomes ridiculous! You've done many things right. What we're after here is a fresh look at change.

If you have set your jaw in a hard line and refuse to acknowledge that change is possible, then the recovery road for you as parents is going to be very rocky indeed! One of the goals that you must keep before you is the one that says, "I don't want this to happen to me *again!*"

Knowing what you've hopefully already learned about the disease, about its possible genetic transmission through your family, you might very well have another alcoholic or alcohol abuser among your kids! This is the time, therefore, to look at change. It is the time to investigate what the replacement of material things with nurturing qualities might do for you as a family recovering together!

If your young alcoholic has been in attendance at AA and at group therapies, he or she will already have learned the value of the "warm fuzzy," that wonderful old bear hug of the variety that passes between people who are *sharing a common affliction.*

Would this be so hard for you to adopt as parents in dealing with your children, with *each other?* How great it is to share a "warm fuzzy" without any suggestion of anything sexual, foreboding, or threatening! It is simply one method that alcoholics and those who love them can use to say, "Hey! I'm here! I *care* about you and about what *happens* to you."

Does that seem so hard to bring into your "parenting process"? One of my daughters uses a phrase with me that has become a standby for nurturing between us. She tells me that she needs me to have my "daddy wings" on or that she can feel when my "daddy light" is on!

For her, it doesn't matter that she is a young adult and that we lead totally separate lives. There are times when she wants nurturing, when she requires me, her father, to reach out as the special person who has always been "daddy." She can be a tough professional, making her own way in her own sphere of influence, but there are times when she *demands* and is not afraid to ask for me to turn on my "daddy light" or put on my "daddy wings"!

So often the alcoholic has reached out time and again for someone to be there—someone he or she desperately wants to love openly and wants to receive love from in return. More than likely that someone is you, the parent, but convention, family rules, and outdated methods of behavior have stood in the way.

When the bottle replaces human nurturing with chemical nurturing, it becomes very difficult to convince the abuser that things can be OK without the alcohol. This was the premise for my book *The Joy of Being Sober* (Contemporary Books, Inc., 1984)—a book designed to show the celebration of life *without* alcohol. There truly is joy in being sober for a lifetime, but to the young person just beginning the hard road toward that sobriety, taking alcohol away is next to cutting out his or her heart!

The alcohol abuser didn't need very much encouragement to pass that scary high school or college test—maybe just a little "nip or two" from the vodka bottle hidden in the locker to "kinda relax" before the test. And it worked! It always provided the nurturing, the comfort, the unspoken phrase "I won't let you down—trust me!" It's almost like a siren's call, and when your young person first heeds that call, it is very difficult indeed to turn back.

Let's look at a list of things that you parents might consider as a start toward either reestablishing nurturing or starting from scratch to begin the process:

1. Begin to institute the "warm fuzzy" between *all* family members. It will seem awkward at first, but try it!
2. Start the regular practice of sitting down *without* other distractions (TV, music, pet dogs, etc.) and spend ten minutes just talking to each other. (It's harder than you think!)
3. Begin to plan some real old-fashioned family activities that you may have thought were "too old" to use anymore. Such things as picnics and visits to the museum or the zoo are ideal events. Sure, these were things that may have been done when your children were little. Do them again! They're still fun!
4. Play a board game again! Take a risk and *ask* your young person. You'll be surprised at how long they've wanted to take up such family activity!

5. Shut off the TV and go to a movie! (You know, a place where you have to wait in line, pay outrageous prices for popcorn, and maybe forget smoking for an hour or two.) Why go? Because you'll be in *closeness* for a time!

These are just five simple things that you can begin to use to make simple nurturing a part of your everyday life. The most important is the easiest and the cheapest: the exchange of a "warm fuzzy," which can be a hug between father and son, between mother and daughter, and all other combinations!

When people are completing therapy with me, it's a natural part of my "goodbye" to give them a "warm fuzzy." I care about them, and I want them to care about me! It is a common bond that will be cemented over and over, no matter where in the world we all travel.

For you to greet your son or daughter, your husband or wife in this fashion is an expression of the old TLC (tender loving care) that human beings need to survive. Its importance to the recovery of the alcoholic is even more pronounced. Nurturing is a medium for saying, "We can get through this ordeal together, as parents and child!"

Whatever has happened in the past just doesn't count, *unless you make it count*. If you, Mom and Dad, continue to focus on what went wrong instead of on what went right, then, of course, nurturing is going to be difficult for you. You can spend a lot of time, as we discussed in Chapter 6, never letting yourselves or your young adults "off the cross."

All of your energy can be spent in going back over old territory, blaming yourselves and where you "went wrong." What good does that do? Forget the old tapes! Begin to make it a practice to reward yourselves by practicing these simple little things we have been talking about as tiny chinks in the armor that may have been building up between you and your young alcoholic.

You both have a lot of anger to get rid of! You, as parents, are angry that you have to deal with this alcoholic, whom you love so much; the alcoholic is angry that she can no longer drink, angry that she can no longer turn to her "friend" and find the peace, the courage, the solace, the love, the *understanding* that it has provided in the past!

Ask yourselves what you *most* would have wanted from your own parents, if it were possible to receive anything. Would it be material things? Perhaps it would. God knows very few of us would not like the opportunity to be better off materially, but is that what you *really* miss in the reliving of your own childhood? I think not! Rather, the times spent with loving parents who unashamedly dispensed hugs and kisses—not just for rewards but for the sheer *joy* of it—would top most lists!

I think of the refined and dignified southern lady who described what was considered "proper southern behavior" with respect to her parents. Oh, how she missed the warmth of being in her father's arms, something that was denied her by her father, who was anxious to preserve his traditional dignity instead of sharing his fatherly love! For her, that was a wish that could never be fulfilled, but she could avoid the same pitfall with her own daughter.

The bumper stickers that are all over America, and the one that inspired the title for this chapter, "Have You Hugged Your Kid Today?" are more than just catchy slogans. For the alcoholic young person that hugging is more than symbolic; it is the fruit of sobriety, the salve for the pain that the family is experiencing now, in the early stages of dealing with the disease.

We think of it as natural to hug, to kiss, to share an outward feeling on all the *joyous* occasions that fill our lives. What about applying the same criterion for the *trying* times of our lives as parents and children, the times that cry out for a togetherness and a feeling of *belonging*, one to another?

That criterion is need! I need to be loved! I want to share my love with you as a symbol of faith in your sobriety!

18

• • •

Sitting
in the
Bay Window

We've come a long way, you and I! From the very beginning
of this book you have had to face a harsh reality; namely,
that you have no power to keep your young alcoholic
sober! You have been using guilt, blame, shame, anger, and,
most of all, denial, as vehicles to avoid taking positive
action to help the alcohol-abusing young person in your
life.

But that's all over! We have discovered that there are new
tools, new ways to get the job done, and new ways to look
at the disease of alcoholism. By looking at alcoholism
realistically, you can approach the problems in a way that
allows the family to *recover together!*

As soon as you are able to leave the guilt trip behind and
get on with the business of getting well, you are making
giant strides in leaving your perch in your own "bay
window." The importance of not getting discouraged cannot be overemphasized. There *are* going to be setbacks!

There *will* be failures! But as parents you have always spent that part of the child-rearing process in learning to pick yourself up, dust yourself off, and start all over again! Treating this disease of alcoholism is not really much different.

Sometimes you will think that you have taken three steps backward for every step forward. It will seem so dark sometimes that you wonder if the dawn will ever break again. But it will! You parents must learn to *trust the process!*

This process requires the complete acceptance of the fact that you have been doing so much enabling that the alcohol-abusing young person has really had *no* experience with the consequences of his or her alcoholic behavior. Mom and Dad have been so quick to pick up the pieces after the damage has been done that there never is any lasting impression of exactly how much havoc is being spread around the family by the alcoholic.

It's only when the family gets help, comes into treatment at one place or another, that they begin to see what they have done in the past and what must be done in the future. There is much joy in watching parents discover the new-found luxury of not having to *accept* responsibility for their young person's drinking behavior!

The parents who are truly interested in leaving the bay window will approach the alcohol problem in a sensible, reasonable manner. There is nothing to be gained by tearing one's hair, ranting and raving, and generally shouting for all to hear, "What in God's name have I done to deserve this?" When the answer is clearly embedded in your brain that you *haven't done anything* except perhaps be a carrier of a genetic trait, then you can get on with the use of new tools for dealing with the alcoholic.

Work hard and diligently in drawing up the contract that we discussed. Make an even *stronger* effort to carry out the terms of such a contract, being fully prepared to carry out the consequences that have been established for breaking the terms of the contract. You will find new strength in realizing that saying "no" and meaning it is not hateful, harsh, or hazardous to the young person's health!

What has to be stressed over and over is your part in the recovery process. You are doing everything that we have written about because you love! It is the very basis of love that makes it so hard for you to stick to your guns! You may want so desperately to relax the rules of conduct, to give in just a little bit or to do some other enabling that will only delay the get-well process.

Don't give in! There will be times when it all seems so logical—when the excuses you are hearing, or the reasons being given, seem to fit in all the right places. But they don't! The alcoholic is a cunning creature, even if he or she is your own flesh and blood!

As the first step of the AA program admonishes, alcoholics are "powerless over alcohol; their lives have become unmanageable!" Your enabling and constant dealing with the issues on the strength of your own personal guilt only feed this lack of management in the alcoholic's life.

Helping your young abuser means *not* enabling! It means *not* taking the responsibility for sobriety away from your alcoholic. What you must do, as we have stressed, is make it possible for everyone in the family to use the tools of recovery.

There is no substitute for family therapy involving mother, father, siblings—the whole kit and caboodle! For all to be involved in the various AA, Al-Anon, Ala-Teen, and even Ala-Tot programs means a family is making a commitment to lifelong sobriety!

Aftercare is to become and remain the most essential part of the process of getting well. Where you obtain aftercare is entirely up to you, but it is something that *must* take priority!

What makes this important? It takes time to process all the adjustments you have made in your life to alcoholism as a disease and to cut off the long-term denial of this problem. It just won't happen overnight, and involvement in some kind of structured aftercare will help this processing.

Parents often tell me that it "seems like a bad dream" and they believe they might "wake up and find it gone." But they won't! And the sooner that *acceptance* of the alcohol problem settles in, the sooner the family can move off that square and into the "victory circle."

It would be to your benefit to make plans for aftercare before you have completed whatever treatment program you may be going through. If you have been working with a public program, the professionals running it will help you find a good continuing group. AA and Al-Anon, it goes without saying, should be kept up on a regular basis, to continually strengthen the resolve to stay sober that has been made by your alcoholic and you.

The unreasoning *fear* that has engulfed your lives should be replaced with a thorough understanding that you are dealing with a treatable disease. While there is no cure, there is much hope for happy, fulfilling lives that are no longer centered around the use of alcohol.

The endless merry-go-round that you have been on, that carousel that just keeps spinning without going anywhere, needs to come to a complete halt! When you learn to give up your enabling practices, a good feeling will engulf you. You will feel a large burden lifted from your shoulders and a new resolve to put your energies to work for recovery instead of guilt and blame-taking!

There is absolutely no reason for you to rehash all the old material about where the alcohol problem originated in your family; it will just be an excuse to mire down in old tapes and not forge ahead to protect other family members.

Did I say *protect?* Absolutely! There are other family members who need to be *fully aware* that the alcoholic problem has surfaced in the family. It may have been years since anyone was identified as an alcoholic. Other siblings, perhaps cousins, aunts, or uncles, have been suffering from the disease, and, perhaps like you, they kept it undercover.

To continue to try to hide such a thing can only force other members of your family to do their own "sitting in a bay window." The alcohol problem—where it came from (genetics), what to do about it (treatment/AA), and how to maintain sobriety (aftercare, AA)—are all topics that should be handled by concerned families.

At a typical family reunion picnic, with everyone gathered around the big redwood table, an alcoholic of my acquaintance suddenly rapped for attention with his fork on a glass. This young man chose this rather inauspicious occasion to divulge his alcoholism before the uncles, aunts, and younger cousins gathered for the picnic.

It was a brave and a bold stroke. As he described it, everyone "just kinda dropped their jaws and looked down" as if Randy the alcoholic had just opened a closetful of family skeletons! He told me it took every bit of control that he had to bring it off, but gradually, and for a period of perhaps thirty or forty minutes, this young recovering alcoholic unfolded his story of what had happened to him.

His parents, wonderful people who had helped keep that closet door firmly closed, took courage from their son's disclosure. They began to elaborate on *their* part in Randy's recovery program—how they had been on their own guilt trips, and how they had come to understand and deal with their own blame-taking and enabling.

Their counterparts around that table were absolutely stunned! Here were the family matriarch and her spouse talking about something that many other family members had suspected but never openly confronted! They were actually *talking* about Randy's "drunkenness," his "weird behavior," etc.! Randy's parents told us in group that it turned out to be a "real experience!"

Randy himself described the disclosure as a "mind blower," with his young cousins asking very intelligent questions about their own alcohol usage and sometimes abuse. What began as a single act of courage on Randy's part turned into an afternoon of the family tracing their own roots of possible genetic predispositions to alcoholism. What had been obviously taboo for this family turned into positive action to identify, encourage, and *understand* not only what Randy was doing but what they themselves might have to do, if alcoholism or frequent alcohol abuse by *any one of them* entered *their* family picture.

So, come on, parents! Climb out of your bay windows! There is hope in your lives—not only for you as parents but definitely for your young person afflicted with the disease! Instead of sitting in the bay window, hoping against hope, you can be active participants in the wonderful process of leaving old tapes behind and playing new ones—tapes that speak of getting well, of staying well, of living well!

For all of you who claim the title *parent,* the bay windows of your lives must allow sunshine to stream through instead of the gloomy and black, despairing rays of ignorance and inaction, of guilt, shame, fear, and denial that have kept you from being whole!

Climb *out* of the bay window! Climb *into* the world of recovery!

Index